OPEN MOUTH, INSERT FOOT

A TEEN DEVOTIONAL

OPEN MOUTH, INSERT FOOT

A TEEN DEVOTIONAL

WRITTEN BY:
STEPHEN WINTERS

EDITED BY:
JOANNA DAVIDSON-BRUNK

TATE PUBLISHING & *Enterprises*

TATE PUBLISHING
& Enterprises

Open Mouth, Insert Foot
Copyright © 2006 by Stephen Winters. All rights reserved.
Visit www.tatepublishing.com for more information.

Scripture quotations marked "NLT" are taken from the New American Standard Bible ®, Copyright © 1960, 1962, 1963, 1968, 1971, 1972, 1973, 1975, 1977, 1995 by The Lockman Foundation. Used by permission. All rights reserved.

Scripture quotations marked "NASB" are taken from the New American Standard Bible ®, Copyright © 1960, 1962, 1963, 1968, 1971, 1972, 1973, 1975, 1977, 1995 by The Lockman Foundation. Used by permission. All rights reserved.

This book is designed to provide accurate and authoritative information with regard to the subject matter covered. This information is given with the understanding that neither the author nor Tate Publishing, LLC is engaged in rendering legal, professional advice. Since the details of your situation are fact dependent, you should additionally seek the services of a competent professional.

Book design copyright © 2006 by Tate Publishing, LLC. All rights reserved.
Cover design and Layout design by Elizabeth Mason

Published in the United States of America

ISBN: 1–5988667–9-6
06.11.01

In loving memory of the American heroes on board United Flight 93—*"Greater love has no one than this, that one lay down his life for his friends." (John 15:13—NASB)*

ACKNOWLEDGEMENTS:

Joanna Brunk-Davidson – thank you for your countless hours editing my work and encouraging me to persevere through the dark times. Little Cassie – 7,942 and counting. To all my friends at Cascade – Joseph Witzig, Shawna, Jen Koski, Kristi Brady and everyone else (you know who you are) – your friendships mean the world to me, perhaps more than I showed – thank you....Simone – my original encourager, thanks! My family – I love you all very much! Dana Barbarick, Steve Browning and family – your stories have inspired me beyond words. My various church families through the years: Rolling Hills, New Heights, EV Free HB, Central Baptist, and Faith Baptist (James Scheller, you rock!) – thank you for the years of instruction, life lessons, and good times. Stephen D. – maybe you know, maybe you don't – you are one of my heroes and I will forever look up to you (ha, literally!). My Australian friends – I love you guys. Jennifer Hoadley – no matter what happens, I'm blessed to have you in my life. God is just starting with you and the sky is the limit....thank you for everything that you are. Cat, Jessi, Kindra – you are three shining examples of great friends. Christal, Darla, and Shannon – you are the original friends to show me what Christianity is all about. Thank you and...I miss those days. Pastor Dave – you're an inspiration to me and I'm glad I can list you among my friends. Alison Strobel – thank you, I've enjoyed working with you on this project! To everyone who endorsed and worked on this book – thanks!

✪ TABLE OF CONTENTS ✪

FOREWORD:

- NOT A TWO PARAGRAPH BLURB, BUT AN IN-DEPTH DISCUSSION OF THE CHRISTIAN LIFE
- QUESTIONS THAT MAKE YOU THINK INSTEAD OF REGURGITATING WHAT YOU'VE READ
- CONVERSATIONAL & HUMOROUS
- DOESN'T CLAIM TO HAVE IT ALL FIGURED OUT, AND POINTS OUT HIS OWN SHORTCOMINGS
- CHALLENGES BUT DOESN'T CONDESCEND

As a high school student, I knew that my relationship with God was missing something. Even though I'd been a Christian for nearly my entire life, there were others newer to the journey that had more passion and depth in their faith than I'd ever had. They all talked about their "quiet time" with God and how they were doing this Bible study or that devotional, and I decided I must be reading the wrong thing. Off I went to my local Christian bookstore to see what else I could find.

Book after book looked exactly the same: short little daily readings that were supposedly meant to infuse some zeal into my faith—and apparently in less than five minutes, since that's how long it took me to finish them. Some of them tried to come across as hip and cool, but left me with the impression that the writer didn't actually know anyone my age and had picked up the current lingo from bad teen movies. The questions they asked rarely required any brain power at all, much less soul-seeking. And more often than not, I got the impression the writer was addressing me from somewhere outside my problems and obstacles because he or she had no idea what my problems and obstacles actually were. I left the store empty-handed and more discouraged than before.

Fast-forward a decade or so. Behind me are years of stupid mistakes made while blundering along the path of life with a sketchy (and sometimes non-existent) relationship with God. Ahead of me is a life that will always bear the scars of those missteps and wasted years. And in my hands is the devotional I wish I'd had back then—and it's in your hands, too.

Now, I'm not going to claim that the lack of a good devotional is the only reason I screwed up during high school and college. Obviously my choices were *my* choices; I was no dummy, I knew right from wrong, and I had a lot of resources at my disposal to help me in my walk. But it definitely wouldn't have hurt to have had a guide like this one. A book that was this conversational and challenging with this much humor and honesty would have caught my eye, and the thought-provoking questions that encouraged me to examine my heart and life instead of just asking me to regurgitate what I'd read would have kept my butt in the chair a lot longer than those brainless five minute blurbs. In a nutshell, I might have finally "gotten it."

If you're looking for a devotional that won't let you get off easily, but will make you examine yourself and your faith, that is written by someone who really *does* remember what it's like to be where you are, and that touches on the struggles, frustrations, and obstacles of life, then don't leave the bookstore empty-handed. Take Stephen Winters with you and pray that God will use him and this book to help you become the person He wants you to be.

~Alison Strobel,
author of *World's Collide* and *Violette Between*,
daughter of best-selling Christian author Lee Strobel

iNTRODUCTiON

My name is Stephen. I'm twenty-five years old. I'm no longer a virgin. I've stolen. I've cheated. I've lied. I've lusted. I've gossiped. I've committed murder in my heart. I've let the sun go down upon my wrath. I've been guilty of uncontrollable anger. I'm a sinner—I've been redeemed . . .

It's so easy to get stuck thinking we are the only ones that have failed. We get lost in the guilt of our own failures. You know what combats this? Grace; it's a simple word with a powerful impact. Have you ever noticed how the Bible is filled with stories of grace? David was an adulterer and murderer. Saul, later to become Paul, was a murderer. Abraham sold his wife into slavery—twice. God used people who failed just like us to do great things.

Luke 12:48b says, "Much is required from those to whom much is given, and much more is required from those to whom much more is given." I can't remember very many times I was more impacted by a passage than when I heard those words in a message—one verse summed up exactly how I'd been feeling. I realized just how blessed I was to have my life, my health, my family, a Savior, my freedom, my future and more. With all that, though, I have a responsibility to use the gifts He's given me to better His kingdom. The burden I feel is huge, but knowing He is in control and I can cast my cares upon Him is sufficient for me. The honor of serving Him far outweighs any so-called demands I feel He places on me.

How about you? What is God to you right now? Do you feel blessed to be here—to be chosen by Him? Yes, you were chosen by

Him—whether you want to admit it or not. You were chosen to live and grow up the way that you have. He guided you to read this book. What do you hope to get from it? My desire is that these questions and many more will be answered for you by the time you finish this book.

As you read, my suggestion is to try to get as much out of this book as you can by keeping an open mind and being willing to learn. The basic format is: a daily story, poem, quote, joke or verse (if they're not attributed to someone, they are stories from my own life); followed by a discussion, some interactive questions, and journal space. I want to encourage you to be as honest as you can in the journal—it's very therapeutic to put your thoughts down on paper! Some of the topics covered in this book may not apply to you but I caution you to stay away from that attitude. There is always something to be learned when God is the one teaching. Finally, all the Bible passages that are quoted in this book come from the New Living Translation Bible, unless otherwise indicated.

Remember, I'm no expert. I'm just a sinner saved by grace and I want to share what I have learned with you. My hope is that I can say the things that few authors are willing to say in a way that you will understand and want to apply to your life.

Why *Open Mouth, Insert Foot* for a title? I can remember "sticking my foot in my mouth" so many times as a kid. It has seemed like an inescapable theme in my life—one that I'm still working through! The disciple I most empathize with is Peter because he is always doing the same thing!

What about you? What things seem to be a recurring problem in your life? I hope that every time you pick this book up and look at the title it reminds you that there is at least one other person in this world who understands your struggles. You want to know the greater truth here? God knows your struggles better than I ever will and He also offers you the hope to overcome them. If I can get you to see that in the next few weeks, I'll have met at least part of my goal! May God bless you on your journey!

THE 'X' FACTOR

If there was one chapter in this entire book that I would want you to grasp, this would be the one! The "X" Factor—what in the world is that? I can think of no better way to begin this book than by talking about the subject which I'm most passionate. Yes, we are going to talk about the "L" word (love), but probably in a way you haven't heard it before. Few people talk about this aspect of love—which boggles my mind! In that light, it makes this concept revolutionary. In reality, it's a fundamental principle straight from God's Word. Have I got you sufficiently primed? Then let's get started!

THE "X" FACTOR: UNCOVERED

John was being mean—as usual he wouldn't leave me alone. I hated him and all the other jerks who made my life a living hell at school. We were sitting in yearbook class trying to finish some work. To my left was the girl I liked, and she was listening to us talk.

He spoke again. "Haha, when are you going to get some new shoes? Those things are ugly."

"Shut, the **** up!" was my immediate retort.

I heard a gasp and looked up to see the shocked expression on my teacher's face.

"I KNOW I didn't just hear what I thought I heard," and she turned back around. I looked over and saw the same girl turn away in disgust and disappointment . . .

I grew up in a wonderful family and I love them all very much. Nothing I'm about to say is meant as a negative reflection of them. God truly has blessed me far beyond what I deserve!

That being said, I need to start this chapter with just enough history to help you understand why this concept means so much to me. I remember how everyone thought that my family was perfect. Literally, we were known everywhere we went and seen as the family that could do no wrong. "How lucky those parents are to have all those perfect kids"–those are the kind of things people said.

Like any family, we were not perfect people. I can't really speak for the other children (I have eight siblings) but I know that I was far from the person everyone thought I was. I grew up terrified that people would know what I really was. I was scared that I would not meet their huge expectations of me. I have four older siblings and I followed them through school. Everywhere I went I was constantly having to live up to the legacy they left behind. In a nutshell–I felt my life was a sham.

Consider the short narration at the beginning. By that time cussing had become second nature to me as it was such a part of the culture I was around. I'll never forget the look on my teacher's face, and I started to clean up my speech in the coming months. I learned the lesson–there was nowhere I could show the "real me" . . .

No doubt I could paint a better, or even far worse, picture of my growing up experience. Either way, my life was mostly the product of the way I viewed it. I chose to internalize things, which is rarely a good thing. I gave you the background to set up this conclusion–for twenty-some years of my life I *hated* myself.

What do I mean? Simple–I'd never liked the person I was. Being the eternal optimist that I was, I always thought things would get better, but I realized I was tired of waiting and thoroughly disgusted with who I was. Have you ever felt that way?

The greatest lesson I've ever learned is this: I should love myself because Christ lives in me. If you've asked Him into your life then know that He is with you; *inside* of you! There are a few principles that come with this concept. First, I believe it is for His glory that we were created. Consider these verses:

➡ SO GOD CREATED PEOPLE IN HIS OWN IMAGE . . . MALE AND FEMALE HE CREATED THEM. (GENESIS 1:27)

➡ FROM THE TIME THE WORLD WAS CREATED, PEOPLE HAVE SEEN THE EARTH AND SKY AND ALL THAT GOD MADE. THEY CAN CLEARLY SEE HIS INVISIBLE QUALITIES—HIS ETERNAL POWER AND DIVINE NATURE. SO THEY HAVE NO EXCUSE WHATSOEVER FOR NOT KNOWING GOD. (ROMANS 1:20)

Living for the glory of Christ is foundational to what I believe and definitely the perspective from which this book is written. Another concept is the inherent value we have in Christ. If you don't know what inherent means, it's okay, I also had to look it up the first time I heard it too. Inherent is synonymous with words like intrinsic and innate—basically it means it exists as a part of something. In other words, we can't change the fact that God created us and we can't change the fact that we have value as a result of that—it's a part of us.

Matthew 6:26–27 says, "Look at the birds. They don't need to plant or harvest or put food in barns because your heavenly Father feeds them. And you are far more valuable to him than they are. Can all your worries add a single moment to your life? Of course not." We have value because we were created and because He chose us to be in His kingdom if you've accepted Him as your Savior. He didn't have to do either!

Questions:

1. What things about how you've grown up do you think you'll remember the most?

_____

_____

2. How do you view yourself? What "issues" popped into your mind as you read today?

_____

_____

_____

_____

_____

 Journal

_____

_____

_____

_____

_____

_____

_____

_____

_____

_____

_____

_____

_____

_____

THE "X" FACTOR: WHAT IT IS, WHAT IT ISN'T

Dear Lord, I see now what you mean. All this time I thought it was about me. How wrong I've been. It's really about you, isn't it? Thank you so much for calling me to be your child and helping me see myself the way you see me. Thank you for opening my eyes before it was too late. God please help me to serve you the way I know I should . . .

I want to devote today to laying out exactly what I was talking about in the first day—what the "X" factor is, and what it isn't. First, this is definitely not a pride issue, though I could see how it might sound like one. Really, though, loving yourself is not about you at all—it's all about loving Christ who lives in you. When you look at yourself in the mirror you should see yourself as a sinful creature, *but* a sinful creature that has been redeemed and forgiven through His grace. When I see myself that way it makes me want to love and serve Him all the more - the focus then is on Christ.

It's also not about self-esteem. What I mean is that people with self-esteem issues tend to focus on themselves. I should know - I was one of them. I couldn't stand the thought of people thinking anything bad about me. If you learn to view yourself with Christ in you, do you see how these issues start to go away? If this doesn't make sense, don't worry, as you grow in your love and knowledge of Christ it will get clearer.

Thirdly, this concept is not a replacement for prayer and reading the Word. Nothing can be a replacement for that. In fact, viewing your relationship with Christ in the right way can really benefit you by giving you a better and more consistent prayer life, etc.

Let's transition now and talk about what this concept is. The "X factor" is knowing that you have value as something God created and that you are here for His glory. You can love yourself just the way you are. The affirmations of other people mean less because of the affirmation you've already received as a child of God. Essentially, the "X factor" is *freedom!*

I have freedom from unreachable goals. Now, I can live my

life by setting achievable, Christ-centered goals instead of trying to obtain a status for myself that is driven by desiring the approval of others.

I also have freedom from pursuing the world's version of happiness (sex, power, money, popularity, etc.). I could tell you story after story on this one. For here and now, let's just say that between you and me we can agree that none of the things listed, or others I didn't list, can ever really sustain our appetite. With Christ, finding happiness is in a better way–God's way. 2 Corinthians 5:16 says, "So we have stopped evaluating others by what the world thinks about them. Once I mistakenly thought of Christ that way, as though He were merely a human being. How differently I think about Him now!"

The last "freedom" I'd like to discuss is the wonderful comfort of knowing that you belong. Being a follower of Christ means you have a family. No matter what has happened to you in your past, no matter how hard your growing up experience was or wasn't, no matter if you've had a real family or not–God is waiting to take you into His arms and never let you go. Rest your mind on that wonderful thought!

Questions:

1. What things about your past might hold you back from grabbing the freedom that Christ offers us?

STEPHEN WINTERS

 **Journal**

OPEN MOUTH, INSERT FOOT

THE "X" FACTOR: APPLICATION

➡ "NOTHING EXTERNAL TO YOU HAS ANY POWER OVER YOU."
~RALPH WALDO EMERSON

➡ "WHILE WE MAY NOT BE ABLE TO CONTROL ALL THAT HAP-
PENS TO US, WE CAN CONTROL WHAT HAPPENS INSIDE US."
~BENJAMIN FRANKLIN

➡ "YOU CAN CHAIN ME, YOU CAN TORTURE ME, YOU CAN EVEN
DESTROY THIS BODY, BUT YOU WILL NEVER IMPRISON MY
MIND."

~MAHATMA GANDHI

My next question for you is this: how do you think life is executed once we understand this "love" concept? I believe the answer can be found in the JOY acronym: Jesus, Others, Yourself. If we could just learn to live our lives with this general blueprint, we'd be the better for it. Look at what the following passages have to say about this:

➡ "TEACHER, WHICH IS THE MOST IMPORTANT COMMANDMENT
IN THE LAW OF MOSES?" JESUS REPLIED, "YOU MUST LOVE
THE LORD YOUR GOD WITH ALL YOUR HEART, ALL YOUR SOUL,
AND ALL YOUR MIND. THIS IS THE FIRST AND GREATEST COM-
MANDMENT. A SECOND IS EQUALLY IMPORTANT: LOVE YOUR
NEIGHBOR AS YOURSELF." (MATTHEW 22: 36–39)

➡ "AND AS WE LIVE IN GOD, OUR LOVE GROWS MORE PER-
FECT. SO WE WILL NOT BE AFRAID ON THE DAY OF JUDG-
MENT, BUT AS WE FACE HIM WITH CONFIDENCE BECAUSE WE
ARE LIKE CHRIST HERE IN THIS WORLD. SUCH LOVE HAS NO
FEAR BECAUSE PERFECT LOVE EXPELS ALL FEAR. IF WE ARE
AFRAID, IT IS FOR FEAR OF JUDGMENT, AND THIS SHOWS
THAT HIS LOVE HAS NOT BEEN PERFECTED IN US. WE LOVE
EACH OTHER AS A RESULT OF HIS LOVING US FIRST." (I JOHN
4:17–19)

There are a few ways to bring this application into your life. The first concept is the *issue of control.* This issue has two points to it. First, who has the control in our lives? Are we learning to give up the "driver's seat" to Him? This is a daily issue and very important.

Second, is the *distinction between our internal and external environments.* This is something I've really tried to get the youth I work with to understand. *You have very little control over what happens around you.* Things happen–we live in a world that is ruled by sin. God never promised things would be easy–in fact, the Christian life was never meant to be easy.

However, you do have control over your internal environment. The quotes at the beginning of this section illustrate this point. You control how you are going to deal with whatever comes your way. Are you going to be happy? Sad? Mad? Pessimistic? Optimistic? Another important question to consider is: How do you want to be seen by others? Or, how would God want you to be seen by them?

I'm not telling you that everything is going to be super easy in your life if you just learn to love yourself. We will still have sadness, trials, temptations, pain, suffering and more. But having God to help us work through these things gives us such a better perspective on the road of life!

Finally, along with the concepts of freedom previously discussed, *you also have the freedoms of peace, hope, and confidence.* It is easier to hope for tomorrow and have the peace of today. Even better is knowing that you can have the confidence to attack anything in life and to achieve whatever you put your hand to, if it's the right thing. That's confidence–God's way!

Questions:

1. What does the JOY concept mean to you?

_____

_____

 **Journal:**

THE "X" FACTOR: WHAT NOW?

Dear Mom and Dad,

It has now been three months since I left for college. I have been remiss in writing this and I am very sorry for my thoughtlessness in not having written before. I will bring you up to date now, but, before you read on, please sit down. **YOU ARE NOT TO READ ANY FURTHER UNLESS YOU ARE SITTING DOWN, OKAY?**

Well then, I am getting along pretty well now. The skull fracture and the concussion I got when I jumped out of the window of my dormitory when it caught fire shortly after my arrival are pretty well healed now. Fortunately, the fire in the dormitory and my jump were witnessed by an attendant at the gas station near the dorm. He was the one who called the fire department and the ambulance. He also visited me at the hospital, and since I had nowhere to live, because the dormitory burned down, he was kind enough to invite me to share his apartment with him and his three buddies. It's really a basement room, but it's kind of cute.

He is a very fine boy and we have fallen deeply in love and are planning to be married. We haven't set the exact date yet, but it will be before my pregnancy begins to show. Yes, Mom and Dad, I am pregnant. I know how much you are looking forward to being grandparents! I know you will welcome the baby and give it the love, devotion and tender care you gave me when I was a child.

The reason for the delay in our marriage is that my boyfriend has some minor infection which prevents us from passing our pre-marital blood tests, and I carelessly caught it from him. This will soon clear up with the penicillin injections I am having daily. I know you will welcome him into our family with open arms. He is kind and, although not well educated, he is ambitious. Although he is of a different race and religion than ours, I know your often-expressed tolerance will not permit you to be bothered by the fact that his skin color is different than ours. I am sure you will love him as I do. His family background is good, too, for I am told that his father is an important weapons dealer in the village in Africa from which he came.

Now that I have brought you up to date, I want to tell you that there was no dormitory fire, I did not have a concussion or a skull fracture. I was not in the hospital, I am not pregnant and I am not engaged. I do not have syphilis and there is no man (of any color) in my life. However, I got a 'D' in History and an 'F' in Science, and I wanted you to see those marks in the proper perspective.

Your Loving Daughter,
Linda
(anonymous internet source)

Our churches today are filled with what I would call the walking dead. As Christians I think we use the past as our crutch—our excuse to remain mediocre. We think "oh, well we failed once, can't hurt to do it again" or "God won't want me now that I've done THAT!" This is Satan working you over. He's done it to me and so many others.

Why do we allow ourselves to get so down on life? Think about the story at the beginning of the chapter - kind of a funny illustration but do you get the point? What do you think the mom was thinking as she read this? Probably, "Oh, no!" as her heart constricts in terror. Ten bucks says she believed every word of it. Why? Because we expect the worst out of the world. The world is characterized by a general pessimism.

You know what? No matter how bad we think things are they can be worse. No, I am not minimizing what you are personally going through. No doubt there are some tremendous obstacles and trials that are facing many of the readers of this book. However, I do think that we get so focused on our so-called problems that we forget we already have the solutions. In the big picture we must remember that God is in control.

Let's come at this issue by asking another question: What gets you up everyday? Is it classes? You want to eat? Maybe you need to go to the bathroom? Take it a little bit further. If we were placed on this earth for God's glory, then what else matters more than glorifying Him? It's not about your abilities or what you perceive as a lack of talent. It's not about what denomination you come from, what church you attend, what friends you've made or even what you look like.

What does matter? God: one word, one name, one answer. Everything else is second to that. Until we see this, we will never be fulfilling our roles here on earth. What do non-Christians see when they look at us? The biggest complaint I hear is that we are all a bunch of hypocrites. For most of Christian America wouldn't you say that there is a lot of truth in that? I grew up in churches that spent more time renouncing and bashing other churches than concentrating on living their own Christian lives well. How many of us are Sunday Christians? Most of my life I've been a Sunday Christian.

What *should* the world see when they look at us? The word that comes to my mind is *real*. Real people with a real love; a real passion to serve a *real* God. If you take nothing else away from today, please let me encourage you to be real about everything you do. We need to be real about our faith, real about who we are, and real about where we are going. It's better to appear less of a Christian and be growing because we are being honest with ourselves than to be someone we are not. It's not about thinking only on the problems; it's about finding the solutions. God has you, yes YOU, exactly where you are, at exactly this point in time for a reason. Our job is not to second-guess Him, but to find where He will have us serve Him.

We don't do this or we don't do that—but I think often we are most guilty of having a lack of passion. Passion is infectious! So is joy. When passion and joy are coupled together—people take notice! Think about the people in your life. The result of a lack of passion or caring is what John talks about in Revelation 3:15: "I know your deeds, that you are neither cold nor hot; I wish that you were cold or hot. So because you are lukewarm, and neither hot nor cold, I will spit you out of My mouth." (NASB) Deep down none of us wants to be a mediocre Christian. If we are Christians—the desire is there somewhere. I've spent most of my life being a mediocre

Christian. I grew up not really giving much of a rip about God. I was saved when I was seven but when did God become MY God rather than my parents'?

Have you ever noticed how real you are when you are doing something you love? For me it's basketball. In my dreams I'm John Stockton or Magic Johnson. In reality my game is probably closer to Big Bird's. I get very into basketball—usually people have to tell me to calm down. You know what though; most people would agree it is something I'm passionate about. It's something I'm REAL about. Think it through—I bet if you think about whatever it is that you love doing, you would agree that you can't help but let the real you come out because it's something you truly enjoy. I wonder then, how we would look if we'd just apply some of that to our Christian walk—the one thing we should be MOST passionate about? What real, passionate people would we be then?

You may wonder what all this has to do with love and God's ultimate design. I will tell you. As I see it, God CAN use anyone, but I would say God can do so much more through people that are ready to be used. Do you remember playing the Oregon Trail game when you were younger? You started from Independence, Missouri and your goal was to get to Oregon and along the way you could hunt, trade, cross rivers, and take care of your family. Now picture yourself in the game as you come to one of those rivers. A ferry is crossing and you pay the man money to ferry your wagon across the river. You load your wagon on the raft and he and four other men strain at their oars to push against the flow of the river and get you across. In the middle of the river you look upstream and see another ferry. You are jealous as you realize that ferry is going to get across the river in half the time. Why? Because the ferry is attached to a rope system. The ropes are attached on each side of the river to a makeshift pulley system and the ferry glides smoothly across the water.

This somewhat crude example exemplifies my point. A person who has not learned to love themselves is like the ferry men pushing and pushing against the flow of the river. The joy of someone who has learned to love themselves is like the other ferry. They have attached themselves to the lifeline that is our Lord and Savior. They may hit rapids, rocks, snags, and branches–but in the end they still have a God whose lifeline they are affixed to.

Notice too that in this example God is out in front–pulling us toward Him. Did you know that a sail is not pushed by wind? The wind actually creates a vacuum on the other side of the sail that draws the boat forward. Is this not how our God is though? He draws us to Himself–it is us that push against Him.

Ultimately the only identity we need is the one we have in Christ. We have inherent value just by the grace we received in Him creating us. Where can we take this thought? The acceptance of peers, love–or lack of love–from our parents, validation as a good worker in our jobs–all of these things are secondary to the acceptance we have when Christ is in us. When you learn to love yourself because of what you have in you, everything takes on more joy. No, I'm not saying life is easy–in many ways it could be more difficult as greater love brings greater responsibility (that's another subject we'll save for a later book).

What I am saying is there is fulfillment that is only found in a right relationship with Him. Think of the greatest feeling of fulfillment you've ever known. I've had a few–a winning shot in an overtime basketball game, a triple play in baseball, a bunch of interceptions in one game in football, being salutatorian in high school (yes, it's true–I was a nerd), graduating from college–I'm sure you can think of a few too. Now multiply that by any number and that is what awaits your *daily* life when you learn to love yourself just as Christ loves Himself.

Don't believe me? Look at the life of Jesus. He was ridiculed more than we ever will be but did anything ever disturb Him? He is the one who did the ultimate act of love. You can seek after power, money, sex–anything the world has to offer and it will never be enough. I could relate countless stories in my own life and the lives of others I've known to prove that true. No matter how much I achieved–it was never enough. The fulfillment we find through

Him is the *only* thing that will ever satisfy. Naked we came into the world, naked we will leave. What we've done in the meantime is what matters–what will you seek after?

Questions:

1. What do you think about this concept of the "walking dead"? Do you agree or disagree? Why?

_____

_____

_____

2. What would it take to get you to love yourself?

_____

_____

Journal:

_____

_____

_____

_____

_____

_____

_____

_____

_____

_____

_____

_____

CHOICES

The goal of this chapter is simple–to show you that every choice does matter. Let's begin . . .

CHOICES: YOU'RE NOT FOOLING ANYONE

She couldn't help noticing how attractive and shapely the housekeeper was. Over the course of the evening, she started to wonder if there was more between John and the housekeeper than met the eye. Reading his mom's thoughts, John volunteered, "I know what you must be thinking, but I assure you, my relationship with my housekeeper is purely professional."

About a week later, the housekeeper came to John and said, "Ever since your mother came to dinner, I've been unable to find the beautiful silver gravy ladle. You don't suppose she took it, do you?"

John said, "Well, I doubt it, but I'll write her a letter just to be sure." So he sat down and wrote: "Dear Mother, I'm not saying you 'did' take a gravy ladle from my house, and I'm not saying you 'did not' take a gravy ladle. But the fact remains that one has been missing ever since you were here for dinner."

Several days later, John received a letter from his mother which said, "Dear Son, I'm not saying that you 'do' sleep with your housekeeper, and I'm not saying that you 'do not' sleep with your housekeeper. But the fact remains that if she were sleeping in her own bed, she would have found the gravy ladle by now. Love, Mom"

Forgive me if the humor in the story above is not to your liking. I love humor like this because it's humor I can understand–that

I can relate to. For what we are going to talk about it's a great illustration.

I want to start off today by talking about the word justify. As Christians, we've made a mockery out of the word—and for the same reason some would argue we've made a mockery of the word Christian.

I'll start off with my own life. How is it that at one point in my life I was doing all the "right" things in my dating relationships (reading the Bible, praying everyday, going to church, reading religious books) and yet making horrible choices that started me down the road to places I thought I'd never be? My story is similar to thousands of other Christians. We live in two worlds—our pseudo-Christian world and the "real" world. Why is it we can't live in one world? Why can't we combine these worlds *and* live the way God wants us to?

This type of living is what I believe is being railed against in a verse I mentioned recently, Revelation 2:16—"I know your deeds, that you are neither cold nor hot; I wish that you were cold or hot. So because you are lukewarm, and neither hot nor cold, I will spit you out of My mouth." (NASB)

The thing is you are not fooling anyone—I thought I was, but I wasn't at all. If you are fooling someone, you are definitely not fooling *everyone*. Like the mother in the comical story at the beginning of today's reading, someone in your life is smart enough to figure out who you are and what you are about. Beyond all that, God sees straight to your heart and there is absolutely no way you can ever fool Him. So why do we try?

Questions:

1. Have you been trying to live in two worlds? What can you do about that today?

STEPHEN WINTERS

2. If your friends were allowed five words to describe you, what do you think they would say?

_____

_____

_____

_____

3. If God were given the same task as question 2—what would He say?

_____

_____

_____

_____

Journal:

_____

_____

_____

_____

_____

_____

_____

_____

_____

_____

_____

_____

CHOICES: IT'S NOT BY ACCIDENT

CHRISTIAN PICK-UP LINES:

- Nice Bible.
- I would like to pray with you.
- You know Jesus? Hey, me too!
- God told me to come talk to you.
- I know a church where we could go and talk.
- How about a hug, sister/brother?
- Do you need help carrying your bible? It looks heavy.
- Christians don't shake hands; Christians gotta hug!
- Did it hurt when you fell from Heaven?
- What are your plans for tonight? Feel like a Bible study?
- I am here for you.
- The word says "Give drink to those who are thirsty, and feed the hungry." How about dinner?
- You don't have an accountability partner? Me neither.
- You want to come over and watch the 10 commandments tonight?
- Is it a sin that you stole my heart?
- You know they say that you have never really dated, until you have dated a Christian!
- Would you happen to know a Christian man/woman that I could love with all my heart and wait on hand and foot?
- Nice bracelet. Who would Jesus date?
- Do you believe in Divine appointment?
- Have you ever tried praying at a drive-in movie before?
- (For the ladies) Excuse me, I believe one of your ribs belongs to me.
- My friend told me to come and meet you, he said that you are a really nice person. I think you know him. Jesus, yeah, that's his name.

~unknown source

You might be wondering how I'm going to relate Christian pick-up lines to the topic of choices. Me too! Just kidding—well maybe. It is similar because it has to do with dating and dating is all about choices, but that is an issue we're going to get to later. Plus, these were just too funny to not include. . . .

On a serious note though, the topic of choices is very important. Today is the last day we're going to spend on it in this chapter, though the concepts we're talking about play a role in everything else this book is going to discuss.

There are four truths about choices that I want to discuss today. First, *being told and knowing the right things doesn't always mean you will make the right decisions.* I've been taught the right things by a variety of people my entire life, yet there have been periods of my life where I screwed up over and over again. However, just because you *might* not make the right decisions, does not mean that knowing the right things has no value. On the contrary, it means that you are better informed, have a better chance of making the right decisions, and have a better chance of making better choices after you've already failed.

This leads to the second truth. *The choices you make now determine the choices you will make down the road.* Do you think the homeless person in the urban ghetto started out saying, "I'm going to be a homeless person! Yippee!" Do you think the President of the United States said one day, "I'd like to be the President" and 'poof' he (or she as the case may be in the future) was?

In my own life, I certainly never wanted to lose my virginity. I didn't wake up one morning and say, "tonight I am going to have sex!" If I've given you any grasp of the environment I grew up in and the expectations people had of me you'd know how comical that statement is. No, it was a series of choices—a progression. Each choice we make brings us closer to sin or farther away.

So what is the answer to this problem of choices that we continually screw up on? There are some obvious ones. Being in the Word and developing a close relationship with Christ through the Holy Spirit is key. Having people in our lives who keep us account-

OPEN MOUTH, INSERT FOOT

able is also key. We will discuss these later. The less obvious answer is to pay attention to the warning signs. Often we will not have a warning when faced with a serious choice, but more times than not we will have plenty of warning.

What do I mean? Are there going to be big bells somewhere and when we hear those bells it's time to pay attention? No, what I mean is that failures, through our choices, are a progression of bad choices and usually we have the opportunity to correct them before they get worse. For instance, a big warning sign for me was when I was asked what I thought of couples living together and having pre-marital sex. This person went on to defend these couples saying that it's better to "try the other person out to see if you will be compatible." I didn't argue but I also did not agree. What did I end up eventually doing? Both of those things, to one degree or another. Does it make sense now? (By the way, this "try the other person out" is a new school of thought creeping it's way into mainstream Christian thought and has absolutely no Biblical basis whatsoever.)

Third, *we need to realize that just because we've made poor choices it does not mean we are damaged goods.* Drug junkies, non-virgins, etc.–these are all people who often feel they are damaged goods, some through poor choices and some through being at the wrong place at the wrong time. It's important for all of us to know that no matter what we've done, how bad we've been, how much we've screwed up–we cannot possible go outside the scope of Christ's love. It's impossible! Ultimate healing is found in Christ and what awesome healing it is too! He has changed me and made me a stronger, better person–He can change you too!

Lastly, *I think it's important to note that even though we cannot go outside the scope of Christ's love, there are consequences to making poor choices.* We cannot expect that everything will be returned to the way it was. Consequences are something we must learn to live with. Think of your own life and the lives of the people that surround you. Personally, I've known recovered drug addicts and people who were sexually active who now struggle with sexually trans-

STEPHEN WINTERS

mitted diseases and other pain. Most of these people are in the ministry now or walk closely with Christ, but that doesn't take away all of the scars.

I give you these examples to give you a picture of what consequences may look like. In one way or another most of you can relate to these examples and you've probably witnessed countless others. There are a host of issues friends of mine have dealt with that I can't repeat in print—but my friends have to deal with the consequences on a daily basis. Sometimes the consequences mean death and / or a choice of separation from Christ.

I want to end this discussion of choices by saying that choices do matter and the best choices we can make are the ones that keep us in line with Christ and His desires for our lives. I'm going to end with two passages from Paul—one of the greatest evangelists who ever lived and a man who has a way of putting things just the right way.

➡ I DON'T MEAN TO SAY THAT I HAVE ALREADY ACHIEVED THESE THINGS OR THAT I HAVE ALREADY REACHED PERFECTION! BUT I KEEP WORKING TOWARD THAT DAY WHEN I WILL FINALLY BE ALL THAT CHRIST JESUS SAVED ME FOR AND WANTS ME TO BE. (PHILIPPIANS 3:12)

➡ I HAVE FOUGHT A GOOD FIGHT, I HAVE FINISHED THE RACE, AND I HAVE REMAINED FAITHFUL. (2 TIMOTHY 4:7)

Questions:

1. Have you ever felt like damaged goods? Why? What has today's lesson taught about that?

_____

_____

_____

_____

2. What consequences of past actions are you currently living with? What consequences have you seen others have to live with?

_____

_____

_____

 **Journal:**

_____

_____

_____

_____

_____

_____

_____

_____

_____

_____

_____

_____

_____

_____

_____

OBEDIENCE

Obedience is a fundamental part of the Christian walk. In a "me, me, me" world it is almost never easy. Our sin nature is our curse—our inheritance from the first sin in the Garden of Eden. Eventually obedience will be exhibited in automatic acts of submission to God's will but first we must, on our own, take the step of faith, take hold of our cross, put on the yoke. . . . then we can proceed.

OBEDIENCE: TO GOD

➡ THOSE WHO OBEY MY COMMANDMENTS ARE THE ONES WHO LOVE ME. AND BECAUSE THEY LOVE ME, MY FATHER WILL LOVE THEM, AND I WILL LOVE THEM. AND I WILL REVEAL MYSELF TO EACH ONE OF THEM. (JOHN 14:21)

➡ SO IF YOU BREAK THE SMALLEST COMMANDMENT AND TEACH OTHERS TO DO THE SAME, YOU WILL BE THE LEAST IN THE KINGDOM OF HEAVEN. BUT ANYONE WHO OBEYS GOD'S LAWS AND TEACHES THEM WILL BE GREAT IN THE KINGDOM OF HEAVEN. (MATTHEW 5:19)

➡ SAUL AND HIS MEN SPARED AGAG'S LIFE AND KEPT THE BEST OF THE SHEEP AND CATTLE, THE FAT CALVES AND LAMBS—EVERYTHING, IN FACT, THAT APPEALED TO THEM. THEY DESTROYED ONLY WHAT WAS WORTHLESS OR OF POOR QUALITY. THEN THE LORD SAID TO SAMUEL, "I AM SORRY THAT I EVER MADE SAUL KING, FOR HE HAS NOT BEEN LOYAL TO ME

AND HAS AGAIN REFUSED TO OBEY ME. (I SAMUEL 15:9–10
NASB)

Above all, we should be most concerned with our obedience to
God–as the first two verses above show us. We also can't be selec-
tive about what we choose to obey; Saul found out the hard way,
as the third verse shows. The Philistines eventually killed Saul and
three of his sons. Further insult was added when Ishosheth (Saul's
son), who'd been crowned king of Israel, was defeated by David's
army. Another example is the life of Jonah. We've all heard the
story of how Jonah was asked to go to Ninevah and call the people
to repentance. The Ninevites hated Jews so this was no small re-
quest. He decided to run away from God and ended up in the
belly of a whale. Broken, he finally agreed to do as the Lord com-
manded. Think of how much easier it would have been for Jonah
if he'd obeyed God in the first place. He would have saved himself
three horrifying nights in the belly of a whale!

The Bible clearly states what obedience is and we know it! Obedience comes in many areas: in word and in deed, in our thought
life, in all our relationships, and also to our government. Think of
obedience as God's "love language." Wouldn't you like to speak
God's love language to Him? Humility, servanthood, selflessness,
obedience–these are things that God must have from us.

Questions:

1. Re-read the life of Saul in I Samuel. What were his mistakes that
eventually led to his death?

_____

....

_____

_____

....

2. Pray now for the things that God is going to teach you as you read about obedience.

⬧ Journal:

_____

_____

_____

_____

_____

_____

_____

_____

_____

_____

_____

_____

_____

_____

_____

_____

_____

_____

_____

_____

_____

_____

OPEN MOUTH, INSERT FOOT

OBEDIENCE: TO OUR PARENTS

My anger burned within me. My dad finally turned to leave and I shot daggers at the back of his head with my eyes. Why did I have to do these chores now? I mean, basketball was on and I really wanted to watch! I could wash the cars after the game. I was a responsible guy—hadn't I proven this?

The Bible says in Ephesians 6 to obey your parents in the Lord, for this is right. In both Exodus 20 and Matthew 19 it says to honor your father and your mother. You probably remember learning these verses at a young age.

Obeying your parents is more than just obeying what they say. Obedience with an angry heart is just as bad as no obedience at all. It also doesn't mean obeying when you feel like it or when you think what they are asking or saying to you is "okay," providing it's not sin. It means all the time, even if we think they are wrong and even when they are gone and can't see you.

Hey, I have news for you. They will be wrong on occasion. They are human; give them a chance to fail once in a while. If God decided to make honoring your parents a commandment, don't you think it was important to Him? Your parents are to be honored for a reason. They know things that we've never experienced before. They've been there and can give us great insight into life if we let them. They've also been given the huge responsibility of teaching us right and wrong and helping us find Him. Perhaps we could cut them some slack!

Questions:

1. Do you think of your parents as young and "hip" or old and "know-nothings?"

_____

_____

STEPHEN WINTERS

2. Identify one area in your life where your parents still hold influence over you.

_____

_____

_____

3. Identify an area in your life that they should still hold influence, but you're not letting them. _____

4. Prayerfully consider talking with your parents about this area and together giving it over to the Lord.

Journal:

_____

_____

_____

_____

_____

_____

_____

_____

_____

_____

_____

_____

_____

_____

_____

_____

OBEDIENCE: TO THE GOVERNMENT

➡ "NOTHING TURNS OUT TO BE SO OPPRESSIVE AND UNJUST AS A FEEBLE GOVERNMENT."

~EDMUND BURKE

➡ "GOOD GOVERNMENT IS THE OUTCOME OF PRIVATE VIR-TUE."

~JOHN JAY CHAPMAN

➡ "MANY FORMS OF GOVERNMENT HAVE BEEN TRIED, AND WILL BE TRIED IN THIS WORLD OF SIN AND WOE. NO ONE PRE-TENDS THAT DEMOCRACY IS PERFECT OR ALL-WISE. INDEED, IT HAS BEEN SAID THAT DEMOCRACY IS THE WORST FORM OF GOVERNMENT EXCEPT ALL THOSE OTHERS THAT HAVE BEEN TRIED FROM TIME TO TIME."

~WINSTON CHURCHILL

➡ "GOVERNMENTS NEVER LEARN. ONLY PEOPLE LEARN."

~MILTON FRIEDMAN

Many people think we don't have to be obedient to our government if we don't agree with what they say. How very wrong that is! Look at what the Jews had to put up with in ancient times. Do you remember the story of the priests who tried to catch Jesus in a falsehood? They asked him if God was the "supreme being," why should they pay taxes unto Caesar? Jesus was not to be swayed. He asked them whose face was on the coin. They told him it was Caesar. Jesus then said, "Give unto Caesar what is Caesar's and unto God what is God's."

We live in a great country that gives us wonderful freedoms—perhaps more than any group of people has ever enjoyed. We live grand lifestyles compared to the rest of the world. I once took a trip touring Europe, which confirmed this. How can we complain when we don't like what one elected official says or when gas prices go up fifty cents? What babies we are! I think verses 1, 2 and 6 in Romans 13 speak for themselves:

STEPHEN WINTERS

OBEY THE GOVERNMENT, FOR GOD IS THE ONE WHO PUT IT THERE. ALL GOVERNMENTS HAVE BEEN PLACED IN POWER BY GOD. SO THOSE WHO REFUSE TO OBEY THE LAWS OF THE LAND ARE REFUSING TO OBEY GOD, AND PUNISHMENT WILL FOLLOW. PAY YOUR TAXES, TOO, FOR THESE SAME REASONS. FOR GOVERNMENT WORKERS NEED TO BE PAID SO THEY CAN KEEP ON DOING THE WORK GOD INTENDED THEM TO DO.

You may ask about all the examples in history of Christians challenging the government for freedom? Here are my thoughts. Our country was founded on the ideas of religious freedom. Various religious groups in England did not like that the government interfered and told them how to worship.

We must remember the context in which these challenges were given. In a mad race for riches, "new worlds" were being discovered all the time. Governments wanted people to be willing to settle into these new lands. Most of the religious groups who were fighting for freedom at that time did not want to go. They wanted to stay and "purify" the Anglican Church. When these efforts failed many of them were willing to go, and did go. As a result you and I are here today.

There is a time for dissension and a time for submission. In this point in English history, it called for dissension. Ordinary efforts had not worked and God made it clear to them that they were supposed to come to America where religious freedom could be established. Where we are in history today calls for submission to a government that is everything those religious groups of the past wanted. We have religious freedom and almost every other form of freedom.

Does this mean that we should give up on changing things we don't like? No! Our country has given us many different ways for our voices to be heard. If you don't like something, change it!

There will still be times in today's world where going against the government will be the right course of action. For example, Chinese Christians have to deal with whether to abort their child (as the various statutes of Chinese law dictates) or obey what they know is right. The idea here is that Christians have a higher moral law to abide by. The only way we will know what to do is from the guidance we get from the Bible and listening to God through continuous prayer.

Questions:

1. What do you believe God says concerning obedience to the government?

_____

_____

2. Do you believe there are times when it's okay to disobey the government? _____ If yes, give some examples and then go to the Lord in prayer and ask Him what He thinks.

_____

_____

_____

Journal:

_____

_____

_____

_____

_____

_____

_____

OBEDIENCE: IF YOU DON'T LIKE IT, CHANGE IT

A sobbing little girl stood near a small church from which she had been turned away because it "was too crowded." "I can't go to Sunday school," she sobbed to the pastor as he walked by. Seeing her shabby, unkempt appearance, the pastor guessed the reason and, taking her by the hand, took her inside and found a place for her in the Sunday school class. The child was so touched that she went to bed that night thinking of the children who had no place to worship Jesus.

Some two years later, this child lay dead in one of the poor tenement buildings and the parents called for the kind-hearted pastor, who had befriended their daughter, to handle the final arrangements. As her poor little body was being moved, a worn and crumpled purse was found which seemed to have been rummaged from some trash dump. Inside was found 57 cents and a note scribbled in childish handwriting that read, "This is to help build the little church bigger so more children can go to Sunday school."

For two years she had saved for this offering of love. When the pastor tearfully read that note he knew instantly what he would do. Carrying this note and the cracked, red pocketbook to the pulpit he told the story of her unselfish love and devotion. He challenged his deacons to get busy and raise enough money for the larger building.

A newspaper learned of the story and published it. It was read by a realtor who offered them a parcel of land worth many thousands. When told that the church could not pay so much he offered it for 57 cents. Church members made large donations; checks came from far and wide. Within five years the little girl's gift had increased to $250,000.00- a huge sum of money for that time (near the turn of the century).

Her unselfish love had paid large dividends. When you are in the city of Philadelphia look up Temple Baptist Church, with a seating capacity of 3,300 and Temple University, where hundreds of students are trained. Have a look also at the Good Samaritan Hospital and at a Sunday school building which houses hundreds of Sunday scholars, so that no child in the area will ever need to be left outside during Sunday school time. - "57 cents", unknown internet source

"The last four letters of American are 'I CAN!' Don't ever let someone tell you that you can't do something." Richard S. Shields Chief Warrant Officer 4 (CW4), 24 years United States Army, Retired

Young people today have an attitude that says "I don't really care what happens in this country. Even if I did, I'm just one person, what can I do? Whatever happens, happens." I should know; I had this very same attitude. There is a huge disparity in voting today. Young people just do not feel the need to vote.

I used to feel that it didn't matter if I voted. My thinking was, I was only one person; how was I ever going to make a difference? I also thought that voting was a big responsibility and I didn't want to put the effort into getting to know the candidates better. Did I really want to waste a Tuesday night when I could do something more fun?

When I went to New Mexico my ideas really started to change. A friend I knew in Oregon was already starting to change my opinions but my physics teacher at the college I attended in New Mexico really changed my attitude the most. Together what they taught me has transformed my way of thinking about politics. How can we change the laws and practices of our country if we don't put any effort into doing so? Everyone in this country cares about at least one issue or another. So what keeps us from trying harder?

People complain about the elected officials in our government. My answer to these people is, "You put them there, why are you complaining?" They usually say, "Well I didn't vote," or "I voted for the other guy." If you voted for the "other guy" at least you put some effort into electing the person you wanted to get elected. But someone who doesn't vote has absolutely no right to complain about any law or elected official.

These seem like harsh words, but what I'm trying to get you to see is that your opinion does matter and you *should* care about what

STEPHEN WINTERS

happens in your country. If you think about it, in thirty years *we* are going to be the "old" ones in this country. We need to put the effort in now to get the future we want. Look at what happened in Florida in the presidential election of 2000. They were counting *individual* votes to see who would be president of the United States. You want to try and tell me that our opinions don't matter?!

For so long in my life I was stuck on the fact that I didn't even get to vote for the president. Here is a historical statistic. In the two hundred plus years that our country has been having elections very few individuals in the Electoral College have voted against the majority in their district. What does that mean? Your opinion does matter!

Why have I spent so much time talking about what you might think is a trivial subject? Do you know how awesome it looks when young people are politically active? Sometimes being politically active just means caring about what happens and not being dead to the world around you. Other times it might mean getting out there and doing something about a particular issue you're passionate about. There are a number of things you could do. The easiest way to start is by volunteering a few hours a week to helping your local candidate in their election (by the way, this looks very good on any application—college or job). Listen to the news every once and a while and discover what's happening in the world. For those of you who are not of the voting age yet don't worry, you will be soon. Now is the time to start caring though so you are ready when it is your turn.

When I first read the story at the beginning of today's reading, I was very excited. I've since learned that the story is somewhat exaggerated, but the just of the truth behind it still applies. I challenge each and every one of you today to change your mindset. Realize that your opinion does matter and the world is waiting for you to start caring. It's not a concept that will change overnight in your head—it takes time.

There are three kinds of people in this world. There are those who make things happen; those who watch things happen; and those who wonder, "What just happened?" Which group do you want to be in?

Questions:

1. Besides reasons already given in this lesson, what are some other reasons you think young people might not want to vote? Do you identify with these reasons? Why or why not?

----

2. If you could change one thing about the world around you what would it be and how would you go about achieving that change?

_____

_____

_____

_____

_____

_____

_____

_____

_____

_____

_____

_____

_____

_____

_____

_____

_____

_____

_____

_____

_____

_____

_____

_____

_____

OPEN MOUTH, INSERT FOOT

PARENTS

You may believe that having a good relationship with your parents is a hopeless cause. I'd like to try to convince you this is not true—God's Word specifically says so. For those of you who believe your relationship with your parents is great, that's awesome. Praise God for that blessing. I challenge you to read on, though. Every relationship can use strengthening! For those of you who have difficult situations (e.g. your parents do not live according to the Bible and have treated you poorly) you might need to adapt the teachings of this chapter (through God's guidance) to fit the needs of your own situation. Take comfort in knowing that God knows and understands your situation down to its most intimate details and He is still sovereign, directing your life.

PARENTS: RULES, RULES, RULES!

- "BUT EVERYONE IS GOING TO BE THERE AND I NEVER GET TO GO!"

- "WELL, YOU CAN GO TO ANOTHER PARTY. I DON'T WANT YOU AT THIS PARTY BECAUSE THERE IS NO SUPERVISION. YOU KNOW I DON'T APPROVE OF THAT."

- "YEAH, BUT KYLE'S OLDER BROTHER WILL BE THERE."

- "ALL THE MORE REASON FOR YOU NOT TO GO. I DON'T WANT YOU DRINKING."

- "I WON'T DRINK AND YOU KNOW THAT! YOUR RULES STINK!"

- "MAYBE SO, BUT I'M YOUR FATHER AND WHILE YOU LIVE UNDER MY ROOF YOU'LL FOLLOW MY RULES."

I was born into a big family. When I say big, I mean big! I have four brothers and four sisters. Most of the time it was a lot of fun being in a big family. You always had someone to play with and there was always good drama.

Along with a big family came a lot of rules. At least that's what I thought at the time. As I grew up the rules seemed numerous: Do your chores and your homework before you go play. Don't talk back to your father or your mother. Don't fight with your brothers and sisters. Play nice or don't play at all. Be on time to everything. Always finish any job you start. Mind your bedtime every night. Don't talk when you're supposed to be sleeping. Be in the house before your curfew. The list could go on and on.

From a very early age I can remember feeling as if my family was different than all the rest. It seemed as if all my friends got to go outside and play before I did. They seemed to always have plenty of new toys and enough money to buy candy. They would get paid to do their chores. We didn't—and if I asked my dad why he would tell me that it would make me more responsible.

I was generally a "good" kid. I did what I was supposed to do most of the time. People thought of me as the boy who could do no wrong. Around the middle of my junior year in high school things changed; I felt as if I couldn't take it anymore. What followed was my "rebellion." I wasn't "bad" in the sense that I started doing drugs or partying or anything like that. My rebellion came in the area of my attitude. I was discovering freedom for the first time and I wanted as much of it as possible. For the first time I was doing really well in sports (at least by my standards) and I was cultivating friendships with different people. It always seemed to me like my dad was holding me back.

I remember one prime example. One Friday night I asked my dad if I could stay at school and play a board game with a group of guys. He allowed me to stay and play. I then asked him when he wanted me home and he said he'd leave that up to me. Well at around two in the morning I was creeping into my bed. The next day my dad told me I was grounded for several weeks and I was to be in bed by an exact time each night after my grounding was over. I was so mad; after all, didn't he say he'd leave my curfew up to me that night?

Looking back on that day I realize that my dad was testing me to see how far I would take my freedom. Man I failed! Big time! I'd completely missed the point of what my dad was doing.

My rebellion really never ended fully until a couple of months before I left home. There were times when I hated my dad for different things. He seemed so strict to me. "He just doesn't understand," was the argument always running through my head. Tomorrow we'll discuss the consequences of rebellion. For now let me end with this: do not be in a hurry to gain your freedom. Recently I actually had someone tell me that I was too innocent because I didn't know what a certain piece of equipment used by drug addicts was. I say what's wrong with being innocent? Embrace your innocence—the more innocence you have the less defiled by the world you are. I believe that in each of us, Christian or non-Christian, there is an innate sense of right and wrong. So before you go charging out the door to gain your freedom remember that with freedom comes responsibility, and with responsibility the knowledge and burdens of the world. You have your whole life to live, so why be in a hurry?

Questions:

1. Identify some reasons you think your parents seem too strict.

_____

_____

_____

2. How do these reasons measure up against what you know of the Word of God?

_____

_____

OPEN MOUTH, INSERT FOOT

PARENTS: ADVENTURES THROUGH LIFE

The feeling was exhilarating! How come no one had ever told me about this? The Cessna 152 surged forward down the runway; I was giddy. How was this thing going to get off the ground though? It was so small, how could it fly? But just then we lifted off the ground as the pilot next to me pulled back on the yoke. I watched the ground fall away and realized I was home. What an amazing feeling this was! I thought I was going to be scared to fly in such a small aircraft, but this was amazing! I could see everything up here! Every buck of the aircraft made my adrenaline pump even more.

"You want to take over?" the pilot asked me.

"You kidding? Of course!" I grabbed the yoke, as she gave me a few pointers.

"See that," she said. "You're definitely a natural."

A natural—I liked the sound of that. . . .

Today I want to describe some experiences in my life to you and then relate it to this point: the people around you that you think do not care, very often do, much more than you realize.

At the end of my two years of junior college I suddenly decided I wanted to be a pilot and started taking flying lessons. At the same time I also got a job at one of the busiest airports in the United States fueling large aircrafts. I got to talk to hundreds of pilots—it was so much fun!

It was not long before I decided to apply to a pilot training school in New Mexico and was accepted. I thought I was the man! After all, I'd been working for five years, had my own car, and paid my own bills; of course I could handle New Mexico. I wasn't worried about the money or anything else. God had helped me get accepted to this school so I would just "trust" Him to take care of the rest for me. My parents didn't voice any objections so I thought they must think it was the right thing to do. I was on my way!

You know that God gives us warning signs everywhere we go. Unfortunately we are usually so caught up with what we are doing that we fail to include Him into our plans and miss these signs. When I got a speeding ticket on my way back from one of my drives to New Mexico or when I failed to get a job during my first eight weeks in New Mexico; I didn't head His warnings. Well God soon showed me that New Mexico was not where He wanted me at that time.

Four months later I was in dire straights. I'd been borrowing on my credit cards for months. The job I'd finally gotten was not paying all my bills. I remember a horrible afternoon when I was at home during spring break. It was a Friday afternoon and I was leaving to drive back to New Mexico the next day. I was sitting on the couch calling my three credit cards to get my balances. Then I called my bank to see exactly what money I had to cover my bills. I found that my bank account was overdrawn over a hundred dollars and I had about twelve hundred dollars in bills coming up in the next week or two.

I never felt so alone in my life as I did at that moment. I broke down crying from the pure exhaustion of thinking through it all. My sister happened to come in the door at that moment and she asked me what was wrong. I told her and she tried to comfort me as best she could.

I left the next day for New Mexico. Before I left my parents gave me some money. My sister had explained to them what was going on. On Sunday night in New Mexico my dad called me after finding out from my siblings how bad my situation truly was. During the next several weeks my dad sacrificed and helped me to pay my bills until I could make it back to California. He sacrificed bonus money he was going to use to pay some of his own debts to help me pay off one of my credit cards. I'd never realized until then how much I really did love my parents and how great they were.

You see, my entire life I'd had the notion that my parents really didn't care. I don't remember ever receiving verbal love, affirmation, or approval and to this day I still fight the desire to try to get that from them. You know what I learned on that day though? When push came to shove, and my back was up against a wall, my parents were *exactly* the kind of parents I wanted on my side. Lesson learned. . . .

Questions:

1. What kind of "road blocks" has God put in your life?

_____

_____

_____

2. What do you think He was trying to teach you?

_____

_____

_____

3. Have you ever felt "desperately in trouble"? _____ If so, what was it and did you turn to God or turn from God?

_____

_____

_____

4. Think of a time when your parents were there to help you out of a tough situation. Did you bother to thank them?

_____

_____

_____

_____

_____

PARENTS: PRIDE GOES BEFORE A FALL

➡ "THE LAST TIME I SAW HIM HE WAS WALKING DOWN LOVER'S LANE HOLDING HIS OWN HAND."

~FRED ALLEN

➡ "THERE ARE TWO SIDES TO EVERY QUESTION: MY SIDE AND THE WRONG SIDE."

~OSCAR LEVANT

➡ "HAS GOD FORGOTTEN ALL I HAVE DONE FOR HIM?"

~LOUIS XIV

➡ "PRIDE IS THE MASK OF ONE'S OWN FAULT."

~JEWISH PROVERB

➡ "PRIDE GOES BEFORE DESTRUCTION AND A HAUGHTY SPIRIT BEFORE A FALL."

~PROVERBS 16:18

What I'd like to do now is go back through the stories and use examples to draw conclusions on where I went wrong. The easiest place to start is at the end of the story with the financial troubles I got into while in New Mexico.

The noble side of me would like to tell you that the reason I never went to my parents for help was because I understood that their financial situation was not the best and I didn't want to burden them even more. Some of this is probably true, but the greatest reason was my pride. Ever since the age of seventeen when I graduated high school I'd been so proud of the way I was taking care of myself. God wasn't really even in the picture. I bought my own car (which later I crashed—that's another story), I was going to school and having fun with friends on my own. Even my curfew was starting to be a little more flexible. When I left for New Mexico I had more pride than you could possibly imagine. I was finally out of the house and on my own; something I'd been wanting for years!

The last thing I wanted to do was go crawling to my parents

and admit that I couldn't do it on my own. Many of you probably find yourself in this kind of situation often.

A friend of mine helped me realize that I was probably doing my parents more harm than good by keeping the truth from them. He told me, "Your parents love you and although they sometimes don't say much and let you figure things out on your own they still worry about you. They hope and pray over you and are blessed when you let them back into your life." This statement is so true. Parents do worry over you. Most love you more than anything else in the world and would gladly lay down their lives for you.

It saddens me to think of how many broken relationships there are out there between father and son or mother and daughter because one party refuses to give up their pride and accept the other the way they are. You know the Bible discusses this. It's no surprise to God. Proverbs 16:18 says, "Pride goes before destruction, and haughtiness before a fall." For three long years my relationship with my father was not what it could have been. Pride kept me from bending on so many issues.

I'm sure all of you can think of a similar relationship in your own life. The root of the problem is most likely pride. If you would search the Bible and your own heart God will give you the answer to what's keeping the two of you apart. Before the week is out I challenge each of you to find one person in your life that you have a difficult relationship with. Search your own heart and pray; then confront that person in humility of spirit. If this person refuses to talk to you, that's between them and God - but it is up to you today to do your part.

Questions:

1. Is there a relationship in your life that your pride is keeping you from repairing?

_____

_____

STEPHEN WINTERS

OPEN MOUTH, INSERT FOOT

PARENTS: THEY'VE BEEN THERE ALREADY!

➡ "MY SON, OBEY YOUR FATHER'S COMMANDS, AND DON'T NE-
GLECT YOUR MOTHER'S TEACHING. KEEP THEIR WORDS AL-
WAYS IN YOUR HEART. TIE THEM AROUND YOUR NECK. WHER-
EVER YOU WALK, THEIR COUNSEL CAN LEAD YOU. WHEN YOU
SLEEP, THEY WILL PROTECT YOU. WHEN YOU WAKE UP IN THE
MORNING, THEY WILL ADVISE YOU. FOR THESE COMMANDS
AND THIS TEACHING ARE A LAMP TO LIGHT THE WAY AHEAD
OF YOU. THE CORRECTION OF DISCIPLINE IS THE WAY OF
LIFE."

(PROVERBS 6:20–23)

When your parents were kids bell-bottom pants and tie-die shirts
were cool. Most of us think that was a different time period, a
different era. They couldn't possibly know what it's like to be a
teenager in today's world. After all, they're *old.*

Technology has changed and so has style, but believe it or not
many of the issues you face today your parents faced thirty years
ago. Your parents were still confronted with drugs, with alcohol,
and with pornography. They wanted a car, to be "cool" in school,
to wear the right clothes and act the right way. They wanted to be
seen with the right people and their heart still went pitter-pat when
that person they'd been eyeing for weeks went by. And . . . believe
it or not, they probably felt the same way about their out of fashion
parents—just like you.

The difference in today's society is how much is now socially
acceptable. Sex is everywhere, bombarding you at every turn with
everything from the movie screen to billboards on the streets. Pornography is easy to get and the internet has revolutionized our
world, transforming us into a society that screams "I want it now,
give it to me now, I can't wait five more minutes."

If you think about it, the same thing was happening thirty
years ago when your parents were kids. America was being transformed just as much then as it is today. Thousands of teenagers

packed concert events to hear their favorite rock stars. Drugs were being experimented with in mass quantities all over the country.

But it's still hard for us to comprehend that our parents could possibly understand what we're going through. We think they lost touch on reality around the time they hit thirty. That's what I thought when I was a kid. I figured they just didn't understand what I was going through.

The first step in strengthening our relationship with our parents is realizing they really do know what we're going through. They are not so old that they can't remember or understand our desire for popularity or money. Once you understand this key point, you will make your life so much easier. You won't always misinterpret everything they say or ask of you. You'll find that you are able to have a real conversation with them. Proverbs 6:20–23, written at the beginning of today's reading, affirms this point.

Step number two is allowing them into your life. Don't be afraid to tell them about what's happening. I remember my dad always being saddened by the fact that I would never speak to him. I don't remember having a real conversation with my dad from the time I was a junior to the time I graduated high school. What is it about our culture that says we have to shut our parents out? They have learned life lessons that you and I have never experienced before. They've gone through more hardships and trials than we can even dream of. Believe it or not they *can* contribute to your success. And. . . . just maybe, you will someday call them your friend too!

Questions:

1. What obstacles do you think you face in learning to love your parents as God intends?

_____

....

_____

_____

2. Which ones are self-made and could be overcome by first learning to put your trust in God?

_____

_____

_____

_____

 Journal:

_____

_____

_____

_____

_____

_____

_____

_____

_____

_____

_____

_____

_____

_____

_____

_____

_____

PARENTS: DOING THE "LITTLE THINGS" THAT COUNT

➡ "THOSE THAT WON'T BE COUNSELED CAN'T BE HELPED."
~BENJAMIN FRANKLIN

➡ A MAN WHO HARDENS HIS NECK AFTER MUCH REPROOF WILL SUDDENLY BE BROKEN BEYOND REMEDY

(PROVERBS 29:1 NASB)

➡ A SCOFFER DOES NOT LOVE ONE WHO REPROVES HIM, HE WILL NOT GO TO THE WISE

(PROVERBS 15:12 NASB)

In continuation from the last lesson, step three is to do the "little things" that can strengthen any relationship. I've listed a few below. Some are things I did and some are things I wish I'd done.

Make a point to come home at least 10 minutes before your curfew. The first time you try this you'll completely throw your parents for a loop. They'll think something went wrong. The easiest way for them to give you a later curfew is by always being early on the one you already have. The easiest way to accomplish that is always aiming to be home ten or more minutes before your curfew. Try it and see what happens!

Tell your parents you love them every opportunity you can. I know what you're probably thinking, "Eww, he's getting mushy on me now." I hear you. It used to be very difficult for me to express emotions.

Give your parents a hug once in a while. There's nothing better than a great hug to increase satisfaction in a relationship!

Your family should be one of the most important things in your life. Make time for your family. You will see your friends all the time. If your family is doing something special make time for them. I can't stress to you how important your family is and always should be.

Include your parents in your life. Don't shut them out; let them know what's going on. Most psychologists will tell you that communication is the key to the success of any relationship.

Make it a point to ask them how their day was. We are always so preoccupied on what's happening in our lives that we fail to care about others. We think of our parents as just people that provide for us and that's it, but they have lives too.

Never confront your parents when you're angry. Look at James 3:4–8:

➡ "AND A TINY RUDDER MAKES A HUGE SHIP TURN WHEREVER THE PILOT WANTS IT TO GO, EVEN THOUGH THE WINDS ARE STRONG. SO ALSO, THE TONGUE IS A SMALL THING, BUT WHAT ENORMOUS DAMAGE IT CAN DO. A TINY SPARK CAN SET A GREAT FOREST ON FIRE. AND THE TONGUE IS A FLAME OF FIRE. IT IS FULL OF WICKEDNESS THAT CAN RUIN YOUR WHOLE LIFE. IT CAN TURN THE ENTIRE COURSE OF YOUR LIFE INTO A BLAZING FLAME OF DESTRUCTION, FOR IT IS SET ON FIRE BY HELL ITSELF. PEOPLE CAN TAME ALL KINDS OF ANIMALS AND BIRDS AND REPTILES AND FISH, BUT NO ONE CAN TAME THE TONGUE. IT IS AN UNCONTROLLABLE EVIL, FULL OF DEADLY POISON."

Nothing good can come out of a conversation that's begun in anger. This is something you can apply not just in your conversations with your parents but in all the relationships in your life.

Never let yourself harbor ill feelings towards your parents. You should never confront them when you're angry but you should also not let the day pass before you do talk to them Ephesians 4:26–27:

➡ "AND DON'T SIN BY LETTING ANGER GAIN CONTROL OVER YOU. DON'T LET THE SUN GO DOWN WHILE YOU ARE STILL ANGRY, FOR ANGER GIVES A MIGHTY FOOTHOLD TO THE DEVIL."

I usually go to a quiet place and get my thoughts together. After I know that I'm not angry anymore I know that I'm ready to talk to that person. Remember that in any argument there are two sides and you need to give as much respect to the other person's argument as you do to your own.

Enlist the help of others. Sometimes you can't see a situation for what it really is and you need the insight of others to help you see it in the right light. This is where youth groups and Christian friends are so important. The man in the following passage allowed his pride to keep himself from asking for help with an interpretation. Acts 8:30–31:

➡ PHILLIP RAN OVER AND HEARD THE MAN READING FROM THE PROPHET ISAIAH; SO HE ASKED, "DO YOU UNDERSTAND WHAT YOU ARE READING?" THE MAN REPLIED, "HOW CAN I, WHEN THERE IS NO ONE TO INSTRUCT ME?"

You can see the man's need for intervention, and the same is true for us.

Don't be afraid to be wrong. Many times our pride keeps us from admitting our faults. Don't allow your pride to keep you from doing the right thing.

For all you guys out there, become a gentleman. I don't mean in an "I'm an old person, I guess I should get my cane and top hat now," sort of way. I mean by becoming more aware of the world around you. Nothing says gentleman like a guy who knows how to pull a chair out for a woman or hold a door open for an approaching person. Your parents will take notice when you do these things!

Ask your parents—don't demand!

Questions:

1. Are you willing to do the "little things" to strengthen your relationships? _____ Which ones?

_____

_____

_____

2. Which of these do you think will be the hardest for you to overcome and why?

_____

_____

_____

Journal:

_____

_____

_____

_____

_____

_____

_____

_____

_____

_____

_____

_____

_____

_____

PARENTS: REBELLION NOW MEANS RELATIONSHIPS TO MEND LATER

➡ "THE REBEL CAN NEVER FIND PEACE. HE KNOWS WHAT IS GOOD AND, DESPITE HIMSELF, DOES EVIL. THE VALUE WHICH SUPPORTS HIM IS NEVER GIVEN TO HIM ONCE AND FOR ALL—HE MUST FIGHT TO UPHOLD IT, UNCEASINGLY."

~ALBERT CAMUS

➡ "I'M TOTALLY GOING THROUGH A REBEL PERIOD RIGHT NOW. IT'S SORT OF WANING, BUT . . . ACH, I'M ALLOWED, RIGHT? IT'S OK, RIGHT?"

~CLAIRE DANES

➡ "I WOULDN'T HAVE TURNED OUT THE WAY I WAS IF I DIDN'T HAVE ALL THOSE OLD-FASHIONED VALUES TO REBEL AGAINST."

~MADONNA

➡ "I DON'T KNOW ANY PARENTS THAT LOOK INTO THE EYES OF A NEWBORN BABY AND SAY, "HOW CAN WE SCREW THIS KID UP."

~RUSSELL BISHOP

You can save yourself a lot of time and energy if you work towards embracing your parents now just as you embrace Jesus Christ. I can't impress upon you enough that the more you rebel now the more hardship you will have later in trying to repair that relationship. Most parents will accept you back into their lives. They probably never stopped praying and hoping for your future. But every time you shut them out you are creating a scar. That scar will take time to go away. Some scars are so big they never go away. Do you really want these kinds of lasting reminders in your life?

Until I left New Mexico and went back home to live for a while I never really realized how much my parents really loved me. Sure, it was in the back of my mind somewhere, but I never really thought about it. My parents have done so much for me. Growing up in a large family they were never really able to give us the material things that other people got from their families. My parents feel bad they were not able to help us pay for college or give us all the things we desired. In talking with my brothers and sisters though I can tell you there is not one of us that resents them for that. We all realize what they've done for us.

My parents gave us so much more than money. We learned valuable life lessons at an early age. I count myself blessed to have grown up in the family I did. Proverbs 19:1: "It is better to be poor and honest than to be a fool and dishonest." They taught us responsibility, the meaning of a dollar, respect and so much more. I remember my family had a reputation for being hard workers. My brother worked a weekend job at the church for a year before he went off to college. I was hired right after him at only fifteen (there had never been a worker younger than eighteen on that job before because it entailed a lot of responsibility). When I asked my boss why he'd given me the chance to work for him he said, "If you are as good of a worker as your brother was, you're old enough for me."

I realize not everyone reading this book has been blessed with a good family. Maybe you're a girl whose father beats you. Maybe you only have one parent and they are always working, so you don't really have much of a relationship with them. Maybe you've never known the true dynamics of a family because your parents have divorced and re-married or you were a foster child, bounced from family to family.

I've never experienced these dynamics, so I can't offer you any amazing words of wisdom. It's unfortunate that you've had to live like that. What I can say is that know that the most important relationship you will ever have is the one that you have with Jesus Christ. This relationship can always use strengthening. He is your true friend. God is your true father who will love you more than anyone else in this world can. Try to find a good church to be involved with. These are your brothers and sisters in Christ and they have a huge role to play in your life. Do the best you can with the relationships you do have with your parents. All you can do is try. If you approach any relationship with a true spirit of humility, it's difficult to make it any worse, so what do you have to lose in trying your best?

Questions:

1. List some things that your parents have taught you about life.

_____

_____

_____

2. In what ways do you feel you are rebelling?

_____

_____

_____

Journal:

_____

_____

_____

_____

_____

_____

_____

_____

_____

_____

GROWING UP IN A CHRISTIAN HOME

 Being a Christian in today's world is hard enough without people putting undue expectations on you. Growing up in a Christian home can often make it harder to live a Christian lifestyle. You've probably never thought about your life this way but I believe it is true and I'd like to explore this topic to see if we can't find answers to some tough questions.

GROWING UP IN A CHRISTIAN HOME: GOING UP!

They'd been watching us for quite a while. My family and I were out to eat, a rare occasion for us, and I was going to enjoy it. I didn't like being watched though and this couple would not leave us alone. I had the best view of them; I don't think anyone else noticed their stares. Halfway through our meal they were done with theirs and I was glad to see them go.

They got up and strode over to us. What were they doing? This was not good. I could see them better now—it was an older couple, probably in their sixties.

"Excuse me there," the lady addressed my dad. "I couldn't help but notice what a fine group of people you all are. Are these your children?" She waived her hand around at the six of us.

"Yes, they sure are," my dad said proudly.

"Wow!" she gushed. "What well behaved children they are; they must be such wonderful kids! You really are blessed."

"Oh, well thank you!" my dad replied.

They exchanged a few more words while the rest of us slunk lower

in our seats. It was bad enough being labeled this way at church—now we were getting labeled in random restaurants by random people?

Growing up in a large family had its advantages. I always had someone to play with and I was rarely bored. Being the "younger" one in the family for a lot of my adolescence, it was easier for me to get away with things. In fights with my older brothers, they would often get blamed even if I'd been the one to instigate it (I almost *always* was the one to instigate it!). In fights with my younger sisters I didn't always fare so well. There are also advantages to being raised in a Christian home. You will hear the instruction of the Bible, Christian fellowship is around you always, and you get to grow up in a church.

Growing up in a Christian family can definitely have its disadvantages though as the devil loves to try to mess up good things! Most parents move through life with a false sense of security for their children. They think that growing up in a church makes their kids less vulnerable to the sins of the world. This could not be farther from the truth. While it is true that there are fewer opportunities to stray from our Christian walk, there *are* plenty of opportunities for us to fail. Remember that going to church each week doesn't make us a Christian and even being "Christian" doesn't make us invulnerable.

Why is it that so many pastors' kids out there have grown up to be complete junkies? They grew up in a church and heard biblical instruction. They probably even professed Christ at an early age. The answer is this: Satan will always tempt us with whatever he can. When we put our minds to it whether or not we've been in a church is irrelevant. We will find ways to experiment with whatever it is we want to experiment with. Those are the facts of life; the results of our sin nature.

Another disadvantage to growing up in a Christian home is the pressures that many people put on us. People assume that because we are "good kids from a good family," we can do no wrong. Where in the Bible does it say that "good genes make good people?" I remember so many examples of people assuming that I could do no wrong and then finding out otherwise. Often these assumptions tempt "good" kids to be bad because they know they are not being seen on their own merits and sin is one way they might receive attention.

In high school I remember a time I was in the computer room playing a computer game. A teacher came in and asked me to do something for him. It was after school and I thought he was just being lazy so I told him no. The expression that came over his face I will never forget. His face said, "This kid is supposed to be one of our good ones - what in the world is going on here?"

There are many of these little examples in my life where people had predetermined ideas in their head about who I was and what I was about. They assumed that because I came from the family I did that I was a "good" kid. They never bothered to determine where I was in *my* Christian walk.

I was going nowhere in my Christian walk for most of my life. I became a Christian at the age of seven. The greatest reason for my getting saved was the fact that I didn't want to go to hell. I was a good person by the world's standards, but I never lived like a Christian. Underneath I was lacking a great relationship with Christ. It wasn't until the latter part of my senior year in high school that I started making any real strides in my Christian walk. For the next several years it was a very up and down time. I'd do well for a couple of weeks or months and then slide again.

Growing up I knew I was not where I should have been in my walk with Christ. Everyone around me thought of me as a good Christian boy and I put up the necessary fronts to keep them thinking that way. I was terrified of people finding out I wasn't exactly what I proclaimed to be.

Many of you are probably going through these same traumas. Perhaps you are afraid to be yourself; afraid of what people might think. If they think the wrong things about you then, that is between them and God. What you need to realize is that before you can move forward in your Christian walk it may be necessary to take a few steps back. God is not going to honor you in falsehoods. Be true to Him and true to yourself, this is the only way you can learn and grow. Being a fake will get you nowhere!

Questions:

1. Do you feel there are people in your life who put "undue expectations" on you?_____ Who are they and what are the expectations?

_____

_____

_____

2. Will you consider talking with them about this?_____

3. From a purely Biblical standpoint how is your walk with God?

_____

_____

4. What things are keeping you from moving forward in your walk with God?

_____

_____

_____

5. Are you going to let what others think of you keep you from following after God? (Did not everyone have expectations of Jesus? They thought He would be a king—when they discovered He wasn't what they thought they crucified Him.)

_____

_____

_____

STEPHEN WINTERS

OPEN MOUTH, INSERT FOOT

GROWING UP IN A CHRISTIAN HOME: IS ANYONE LISTENING?

EVERY DAY IS A NEW STRUGGLE,
THE SAME PAINS I FACE,
AND FOR SPLIT SECONDS THROUGHOUT THE DAY,
MY HAPPINESS HAS A FACE.
THOUGH OUTSIDE EVERYTHING IS "PEACHY KEEN,"
DEEP INSIDE THERE IS A HOLE THAT NO ONE HAS EVER SEEN.
WHEN OTHERS FALL I AM THERE TO HELP THEM RISE,
TO HOLD THEM, TO CARRY THEM, TO TELL THEM IT IS TRUE.
THAT GOD LOVES ME AND HE MOST CERTAINLY LOVES YOU.
YET AFTER I AM ALONE, UNDER MY COVERS IN A BALL,
I WEEP VERY GENTLY, KNOWING I HAVE FOOLED YOU ALL.
I SMILE BECAUSE IT BRINGS HAPPINESS TO OTHERS,
BUT INSIDE MY HEART I FEEL THE EMPTINESS OF DARKNESS
THAT HOVERS.
SO THE NEXT TIME YOU SEE ME, DON'T PITY ME WITH OWES.
I AM FINE, TRUST ME. . . . AS FAR AS EVERYONE KNOWS.

~STACIE WILLIAMS, PERSONAL FRIEND

During my teenage years I remember feeling as if there wasn't really anyone I could talk to about the issues that were really bothering me. I was a closed-mouth type of person to begin with and I had great difficulty in discussing serious issues with people I really cared about.

The world often seemed to be moving too fast around me and I just wanted it to slow down. There were so many expectations on me; the ones I hadn't created myself had been placed on me by others such as teachers and people in my church.

In a world where I felt I had no one to talk to I tended to internalize most things. This can be very unhealthy and I don't recommend it to anyone. There were times I wanted to scream because I just wanted someone I could truly talk to. I went to a really small

STEPHEN WINTERS

high school where gossip was the soup of the day and true friendship was hard to come by. In all four years of high school I never had a true friend that I could talk to. The closest I ever came to a good friend was a guy two years older than me who I really looked up to—literally; he was six-foot-five! The best conversations of my entire high school were with him during baseball batting practices and long van rides. I'm blessed to say this man is now my brother-in-law, but that's a love story my sister should tell!

For anyone out there who deals with these feelings of hopelessness please read on! Believe it or not there are people out there who care about you and will listen to you. It's sometimes easier for us to believe that no one cares than to open up to someone, but we must pry ourselves away from this practice. Below are just a few of the people who you might try to cultivate a good relationship with to help you in the issues that you face in life.

GOD should be the first one you go to in times of need. If your relationship with God is not like this, I encourage you to do what you can to get it back on track. God has all the answers and the deeper your relationship with Him, the better you will understand Him and His plan for this universe. Remember prayer is our avenue for conversation with Him.

YOUR PARENTS are great sources of wisdom. I wish I'd known that when I was a teenager. Someone once told me something that I think is both funny and very true: The twenty-one year old told his dad, "Dad you didn't know anything when I was in high school; it's really amazing what you've learned in six years!" Sad, but true. Your parents have been there before and they just might understand what you're going through. Don't be afraid to talk to your parents once in a while.

TEACHERS OR PASTORS are usually great neutral sources of wisdom; they generally will try to give you objective answers. These are also the people often putting undue pressure on you as discussed earlier in this chapter. There is absolutely nothing wrong with confronting them on this issue though. Most people don't even realize they are doing it and will be happy to try to stop. Who knows, you might just find a needed ally.

OPEN MOUTH, INSERT FOOT

Hopefully you have found some great *friends* in your life that you can confide in. It's very important to choose your friends wisely. They can and will have a very big influence on the decisions you make in your life. A good friend will comfort you in times of sorrow and be happy with you in times of triumph. Most importantly they will be growing Christians themselves and not be afraid to gently prod you in the right direction once in a while when they feel guided by the Lord to do so. Proverbs 17: 7: "A friend is always loyal, and a brother is born to help in time of need." For those of you who have found these kinds of friends; consider yourself blessed from the Lord. If you have not been able to find this kind of friend yet, keep searching, they are out there!

Questions:

1. If you were standing before God and He asked: "Do your friends fall under the category of "superficial" or "dedicated friend," how would you respond?

_____

_____

_____

_____

2. Are you reaching out to others who may be struggling to find quality friends?

_____

_____

_____

_____

STEPHEN WINTERS

_____

_____

_____

_____

_____

_____

_____

_____

_____

_____

_____

_____

_____

_____

_____

_____

_____

_____

_____

_____

_____

_____

_____

_____

_____

OPEN MOUTH, INSERT FOOT

GROWING UP IN A CHRISTIAN HOME: A WORD ABOUT INNOCENCE

➡ THEN JOSEPH HAD A DREAM, AND WHEN HE TOLD IT TO HIS BROTHERS, THEY HATED HIM EVEN MORE. HE SAID TO THEM, "PLEASE LISTEN TO THIS DREAM WHICH I HAVE HAD; FOR BEHOLD, WE WERE BINDING SHEAVES IN THE FIELD, AND LO, MY SHEAF ROSE UP AND ALSO STOOD ERECT; AND BEHOLD, YOUR SHEAVES GATHERED AROUND AND BOWED DOWN TO MY SHEAF." THEN HIS BROTHERS SAID TO HIM, "ARE YOU ACTUALLY GOING TO REIGN OVER US? OR ARE YOU REALLY GOING TO RULE OVER US?" SO THEY HATED HIM EVEN MORE FOR HIS DREAMS AND FOR HIS WORDS. GENESIS 37: 5–8 (NASB)

I've mentioned innocence in another chapter, but I thought this would be a good point to bring it up again and discuss it a bit further. I think as a youth growing up in a Christian home there was a certain part of me that longed for the ways of the world. In essence, I wanted to lose my innocence–to really know what it was like out there. I was naïve to the ways of the world and I knew it.

Being naïve isn't all bad though. Sadly I had to discover this through many difficult experiences in my life. After those, I longed to go back to the days of innocence when my biggest problems were getting through a day of school or avoiding my dad when I got home.

I think some of the reason so many Christian youths are falling away from the church is because a majority of them see their innocence as a curse. They see from afar what is going on out there in "the real world" and they want that for themselves. They have unfair expectations on them and see their innocence as a part of that huge weight on their shoulders. I've talked with many others who felt the same way when they were younger. It makes sense doesn't it?

Losing your innocence is the thing I wanted so much and

when I got it I wished I'd never lost it. There are many ways to lose your innocence—but rest assured of one conclusion: at some point every one of us loses our innocence. Whether it is from experience or from seeing it first hand with someone in our lives, the sin of the world is everywhere—it will find you. The question is, what are you going to do when it does?

You see, there is no point in looking for it—it finds you. Joseph found this out the hard way. Read the passage from Genesis 37 at the beginning of this section again. I picture Joseph being one of those snot-nosed, goody two-shoes types. The kind that never does any wrong and you want to scream because they are so "perfect." I've known a few people like that before and it certainly didn't inspire me to do better—they were almost too perfect.

Well, Joseph's brothers couldn't take it any longer and sold Joseph into slavery. I really believe until that moment Joseph had *no clue* what the real world was like. After all, he was his father's favorite son, had plenty of money, and God was giving him some really cool dreams. He was basically on the easy road of life.

You should take the time to read the rest of the story of Joseph. It really is an amazing story of a family torn apart and brought back together again through the amazing hand of God. For purposes of our study here I think it's more important to note that though Joseph lost his innocence and was no longer naïve to the world, God did not forsake him at all. Joseph went through some incredible pain and hard work, but eventually found redemption in the land of Egypt.

What about you? Are you in a hurry to lose your innocence? Are some of your friends in a hurry? Perhaps you might step in and share with them the story of Joseph. Today, I'm not going to ask any questions. I simply want you to think about what we've talked about. Perhaps today's lesson has helped you see your life for what it really is. Perhaps it has helped you understand your world and how you fit into it better. Take some time to think this through and don't be afraid to write in your journal about it—I've given you some extra space today.

OPEN MOUTH, INSERT FOOT

ALIGNING YOUR GOALS

Many Christians believe God has a single plan for each of our lives. They use the following verse as their proof:

➡ "FOR I KNOW THE PLANS I HAVE FOR YOU," SAYS THE LORD. "THEY ARE PLANS FOR GOOD AND NOT FOR DISASTER, TO GIVE YOU A FUTURE AND A HOPE. IN THOSE DAYS WHEN YOU PRAY, I WILL LISTEN. IF YOU LOOK FOR ME IN EARNEST, YOU WILL FIND ME WHEN YOU SEEK ME." JEREMIAH 29:11–13

I challenge each of you to think differently, with the following premise for our lives: God has a *plan* and it's up to each of us to see His plan and find our own place in it. Proverbs 19:21 states: "You can make many plans, but the Lord's purpose will prevail."

Am I saying that God doesn't have one purpose for our lives? No, of course not. He placed each of us on this earth for very specific reasons. First and foremost He put us on this earth to glorify Him. We do that each time we follow Him in obedience. It is very important how we obey, though we spend so much of our time asking God what He is going to bring for us to do, when we should be seeking God's guidance, putting him in the "drivers seat," and watching where He opens up opportunities. We need to move from a "let God bring it to us" attitude to a "go out and find where God is working and join Him" attitude!

ALIGNING YOUR GOALS: DECISIONS CAN BE TOUGH...

➡ "MAN IS A GOAL SEEKING ANIMAL. HIS LIFE ONLY HAS MEAN

ING IF HE IS REACHING OUT AND STRIVING FOR HIS GOALS."

~ARISTOTLE

➡"IF YOU DON'T KNOW WHERE YOU ARE GOING, YOU MIGHT WIND UP SOMEPLACE ELSE."

~YOGI BERRA

➡"GOALS HELP YOU CHANNEL YOUR ENERGY INTO ACTION.

➡"YOUR GOALS ARE THE ROAD MAPS THAT GUIDE YOU AND SHOW YOU WHAT IS POSSIBLE FOR YOUR LIFE."

~LES BROWN

Why do you think it is that most college freshman change their majors at least once - or more - before they graduate? Do you think it might be because God has not told them what He wants them to do? Maybe you think He's just trying to play musical chairs with our lives.

College freshman often change their major because they have failed to consult with God about where He wants them to fit into His plans. I never remember praying to God and asking Him what it was He wanted me to do. I've changed my major and career more times than I can count. I don't think that God tries to waste our time. No, it is our failure to consult with Him that is the problem. Not only must we consult with Him, but we must then allow Him to take control.

Questions:

1. What decision(s) are you confronted with?

_____

_____

2. What's been your approach to solving this problem and in what ways have you involved God?

_____

_____

STEPHEN WINTERS

3. What decisions have cost you something in the past?

_____

_____

4. Did you go to God first?

_____

_____

⟨▲⟩ Journal:

_____

_____

_____

_____

_____

_____

_____

_____

_____

_____

_____

_____

_____

_____

_____

OPEN MOUTH, INSERT FOOT

ALIGNING YOUR GOALS: ACKNOWLEDGE YOUR NEEDS

➡ "ARE YOU A SNIOP? SOMEONE WHO IS SENSITIVE TO THE NEGATIVE INFLUENCE OF OTHERS?"

~ZIG ZIGLER

➡ "GET AROUND PEOPLE WHO HAVE SOMETHING OF VALUE TO SHARE WITH YOU. THEIR IMPACT WILL CONTINUE TO HAVE A SIGNIFICANT EFFECT ON YOUR LIFE LONG AFTER THEY HAVE DEPARTED."

~JIM ROHN

(Continuing from yesterday)

I know what you might be thinking, probably the same thing I was before I allowed God control in my life. "Are you crazy, give God control?" we say. "Then He's going to make me some Bible thumping evangelist–but I want to be cool."

I remember one of my greatest fears when I was a kid was that if I allowed God any control over my life he'd make me a preacher—or worse—a missionary. I was deathly afraid of being sent to some far-off place to wrestle cannibals away from their evil practices. After all, both my dad and my grandpa had been missionaries in Japan (that's where I was born) so didn't that mean that there was a good chance that I too would be summoned for duty?

There's something about being outside the plan of God that scares me. The world is a very evil place. I like the comfort and protection that I have when I'm in my Father's arms; in His plans. Never was I as lonely as when I was in New Mexico. I had no family to comfort me and at times I strayed very far from God. That is a lonely feeling! How good it feels to know that God is always there for us to run back to. You might ask how we can come back to God when we strayed so far. The first thing to do is to acknowledge that we do need help and that we are lost without Him. Until we admit this we are stuck. The next thing we need to do is confess all the things that are keeping us from God. We should be as specific as we can. God already knows our sins but He wants to see if we will acknowledge our need of Him and our failure in the past.

I remember growing up in church hearing these same words. I never thought they really meant much. I always wondered why you had to talk about the past with God. He knows what you've done, and after He died for us on the cross, doesn't He see all Christians "white as snow?"

While it's true that God sees you "white as snow" it is still impossible to move closer to God when there are past sins keeping you from Him. God will take you back with open arms but there will still be that sin keeping you from that true closeness with Him. It's like unspoken wrongs between friends. You might be forgiven, but how much better do you feel when you talk about and move past it together?

Questions:

1. What is your greatest fear about turning your life over to the Lord?

_____

_____

_____

_____

_____

2. What part of your life are you still struggling to give to Him?

_____

_____

_____

_____

_____

ALIGNING YOUR GOALS: MOVING ON

I needed to stop thinking about it. No good could come of it and I wanted to get on with my life. If she didn't think I was the one for her then I should accept that. It hurt, but I'd been hurt before and I could deal with it now. I hit the delete button and turned away from the computer, resolving to try to enjoy the rest of my evening . . .

Once you've confessed your sins it is important that you do not dwell in the past. When you have confessed those sins, God has forgiven you and thinks of it no more. You should do the same. What right do we have to dig up the sins God buried? Don't mock His forgiveness. Let it go. We'll talk about that more in a later chapter. Also, never think you have sinned so badly that God does not want to spend time with you. A lot of people let sin unduly hinder their relationship with God.

Once you've made it a goal to have a genuine relationship with God, then it is important you do everything you can to cultivate that relationship. Make it a point each day, as you wake up, to give your first moments to God. Resolve to spend quiet time with Him as soon as you can. I do it in the mornings right after I get to work because the distractions are the fewest and I'll remember to do it. Whatever time you do it, try to do it at the same time each day. The routine will turn into a habit, and having a habit of spending quiet time with God is a good thing!

Think of your devotions as your fuel for the day. It is the sustainer of the relationship that you have with Christ, the power that will help you to fight the evil that is all around us every day of our lives. You cannot possibly hope to have a relationship with God unless you talk to Him. Would you want a girlfriend or boyfriend, or even a friend, who never spoke to you? Talk to God all the time. In your devotions, on your way to school or work, when confronted by a situation; anytime! The more you talk to God, the more He will reveal to you about Himself and the plan He has for this world. Slowly but surely you will start to realize where you fit into those plans.

Questions:

1. What has been the hardest part for you in trying to start a daily routine with God?

_____

_____

_____

_____

Journal:

_____

_____

_____

_____

_____

_____

_____

_____

_____

_____

_____

_____

_____

_____

_____

ALIGNING YOUR GOALS: PATIENCE

A young and successful executive was traveling down a neighborhood street, going a bit too fast in his new Jaguar. He was watching for kids darting out from between parked cars and slowed down when he thought he saw something. As his car passed, no children appeared. Instead, a brick smashed into the Jag's side door! He slammed on the brakes and drove the Jag back to the spot where the brick had been thrown.

The angry driver then jumped out of the car, grabbed the nearest kid and pushed him up against a parked car shouting, "What was that all about and who are you? Just what the heck are you doing? That's a new car and that brick you threw is going to cost a lot of money. Why did you do it?"

The young boy was apologetic. "Please, mister . . . please, I'm sorry . . . I didn't know what else to do," He pleaded. "I threw the brick because no one else would stop . . ." With tears dripping down his face and off his chin, the youth pointed to a spot just around a parked car. "It's my brother," he said. "He rolled off the curb and fell out of his wheelchair and I can't lift him up."

Now sobbing, the boy asked the stunned executive, "Would you please help me get him back into his wheelchair? He's hurt and he's too heavy for me."

Moved beyond words, the driver tried to swallow the rapidly swelling lump in his throat. He hurriedly lifted the handicapped boy back into the wheelchair, then took out his fancy handkerchief and dabbed at the fresh scrapes and cuts. A quick look told him everything was going to be okay. "Thank you and may God bless you," the grateful child told the stranger.

Too shook up for words, the man simply watched the boy push his wheelchair- bound brother down the sidewalk toward their home. It was a long, slow walk back to the Jaguar. The damage was very noticeable, but the driver never bothered to repair the dented side door. He kept the dent there to remind him of how his impatience had so blinded him . . . "The Brick", unknown author

OPEN MOUTH, INSERT FOOT

I think I've been strayed by the voice of Satan more times than I could possibly count. You might find yourself with the same problem. You want to do what's right but how do you trust that what you see or hear is from God? I cannot offer you any spectacular words of wisdom in this area because I still go through this problem. I probably will until the day I die. What I can tell you is what I've learned through this point in my life.

The easiest way to distinguish between God's voice and Satan's is to simply ask God. This is where a strong, daily relationship with God is so important. The stronger your relationship is with God the harder it will be for Satan to try and break up that relationship and get you to do the wrong thing. Many times you will feel that God is being silent on the issues you face but have patience, the answers are there. If you truly have a heart for doing what's right God will not let you down.

It is very difficult sometimes to wait on God. Most of the time we feel safer when we are doing something. Often times though God is simply trying to teach us patience. I'm probably one of the most impatient people you will ever meet; you can imagine how many times God has tried to teach me patience. What I've learned (the hard way) is that it is easier to wait on God than it is to try and strike out on my own and do it my way.

I can tell you many stories of how my impatience got me in trouble. Like when I got a speeding ticket going through Arizona or how my own desire to go to New Mexico to start flying set me back nine thousand dollars of debt. Impatience is not a good attribute to have. We'd do well to learn from the life of Job in the Bible. Many people like that story because Job showed unbelievable trust in God when everything was crumbling around him. I like the story because Job also showed unbelievable patience in God. How many of us can wait on God like that? I'd probably have been trying to save what I had left, but Job trusted that God would take care of him—and He did.

It may be that you've had a great relationship with God for some time now and He still has not shown you where you fit into His plan. Don't stress! You can serve God anyway. You don't have to wait for specific orders when it comes to service. God has given you a church where you have many opportunities to serve.

Do you know how unbelievably awesome it looks when young people are seen serving the Lord? It is a huge inspiration and motivation to others in the church to start serving the Lord also.

It's easy to be unsure of where to serve or to think we have no talents, but I guarantee you if you have the desire to help, there will be somewhere for you to serve. There's nothing wrong with trying to serve in different areas until you find what you are best suited for. Just give it a shot!

Questions:

1. Are you struggling with remaining patient?

_____

_____

_____

_____

_____

2. Are you waiting on God for something and it seems like He's not answering? (Hint, the right answer is usually the most obvious one!)

_____

_____

_____

_____

_____

_____

 **Journal:**

ALIGNING YOUR GOALS: DATING

Ha, how ironic. This always seemed to happen to me. I could tell a few girls were interested in me, but the one girl I liked didn't like me back. She liked another guy and I thought he was a good guy—so I was okay with that, right? So why couldn't I stop thinking about her? Why couldn't I concentrate on finishing my homework and doing the things I should be doing? What a waste of time. Yet, I couldn't stop thinking about her. I just wanted to find my "someone"—was that too much to ask?

Most of you probably think this is the part where I start dissing what you're doing. No kissing, touching, petting, or sex. If that's what you think than it appears you already have some ideas about what's right and wrong in that area! No, I'd like to ask you a question instead: When you are dating are you honoring God?

God has a place for you in His plan. When you are dating at such a young age you may be altering your place in God's plan. You are emotional attaching yourself to someone else when you should be finding your sense of belonging in God. I believe casual dating, especially at a young age, leads to this giving of emotions.

Although you'll hear different Christians saying different things, I believe there is nothing wrong with dating in high school or college. However, if you're not ready for marriage it's quite possible you're giving away valuable time. When you spend so much time thinking about the opposite sex you are wasting time that you could be giving to God. I remember spending many of my waking hours thinking about various girls at school. I was one of those guys that liked one girl for a really long time and never got over her very easily. Just imagine how much time I wasted thinking about them when I could have been serving God in some manner.

The Bible says in Matthew 6:24: "No one can serve two masters. Either he will hate the one and love the other, or he will be devoted to the one and despise the other. You cannot serve both God and money." (NASB) This verse is referring to money, but the principle still applies. Girls (or boys) are not gods, but they can be too much of a priority. I know I'm touching on a difficult subject, but sometimes the hard things are the things we need to hear.

What we are talking about is something you are going to have to decide for yourself. The world will judge you by your actions and what you pursue, so choose wisely. Also. . . . now is the time to make these decisions, not when it's too late!

Questions:

1. Where do you draw the line in how far the level of intimacy goes in your relationships with the opposite sex (spiritually, emotionally, and physically)?

_____

_____

_____

Journal:

_____

_____

_____

_____

_____

_____

_____

_____

_____

_____

STEPHEN WINTERS

ALIGNING YOUR GOALS: THIS GAME CALLED LIFE, LAUGH OR CRY?

➡ "IMAGINATION WAS GIVEN MAN TO COMPENSATE FOR WHAT HE IS NOT, AND A SENSE OF HUMOR TO CONSOLE HIM FOR WHAT HE IS."

~FRANCIS BACON

➡ "A PERSON WITHOUT A SENSE OF HUMOR IS LIKE A WAGON WITHOUT SPRINGS-JOLTED BY EVERY PEBBLE IN THE ROAD."

~HENRY WARD BEECHER

➡ "WE MUST LAUGH AT MAN TO AVOID CRYING FOR HIM."

~NAPOLEON BONAPARTE

➡ "IF I HAD NO SENSE OF HUMOR, I WOULD LONG AGO HAVE COMMITTED SUICIDE."

~MAHATMA GANDHI

When we look at the world around us we could easily choose to grow bitter. We could throw our hands up and say, "How can we possibly make a difference?" People are murdered on the streets, babies aborted, wars fought, suicides committed, banks robbed, women raped–well the list could go on and on. These days we even have the added discomfort of living with the somewhat new threat of terrorism. If we allowed ourselves to focus on the negatives too closely no doubt we would give up.

You know what I choose to do? I laugh! Before you think me to be making a mockery of tragedy, let me explain. You see I think God has a serious sense of humor. I could tell you many stories in my life of how God has done the funniest things. I can't believe that God is up there all somber faced and serious all the time.

So I choose to use His example. I love humor! I can't imagine my life without the daily joys of humor. Let me put it to you this way: we know the end result, don't we? God has assured us that He will return as our victorious King. If we know the outcome then why not learn to enjoy the journey? Why can't we do His work and enjoy the ride as well? I have no doubt this is what God wants for us. Also, people are attracted to fun people—so let's show the world just how great our God is!

Questions:

1. How do you think the world sees Christians today? Why and how can we do a better job of reaching them?

_____

_____

_____

_____

Journal:

_____

_____

_____

_____

_____

_____

_____

_____

_____

_____

_____

_____

HARD TALK

When I thought about writing this book, discussing the church was definitely not something I was planning to do. This chapter is controversial. In fact, some churches may even ban this book because of what is in it. As you read, please remember that not everything applies to everyone. Instead of becoming ofended, lets try to see what God is teaching us. Whatever happens, I felt like the truths in this chapter needed to be said. . . .

HARD TALK: THE "PERFECT CHURCH"

➡ "IT IS ONLY IMPERFECTION THAT COMPLAINS OF WHAT IS IMPERFECT. THE MORE PERFECT WE ARE THE MORE GENTLE AND QUIET WE BECOME TOWARDS THE DEFECTS OF OTHERS."

~JOSEPH ADDISON

➡ "NOTHING WOULD BE DONE AT ALL IF ONE WAITED UNTIL ONE COULD DO IT SO WELL THAT NO ONE COULD FIND FAULT WITH IT."

~CARDINAL J. NEWMAN

➡ "IF THERE WAS NOTHING WRONG IN THE WORLD, THERE WOULDN'T BE ANYTHING FOR US TO DO."

~GEORGE BERNARD SHAW

➡ "I AM BUT A FOREIGNER HERE ON EARTH; I NEED THE GUIDANCE OF YOUR COMMANDS. DON'T HIDE THEM FROM ME!"

~PSALMS 119:19

Is there such a thing as the "perfect church?" Trick question? Maybe. I don't like the word perfect, but I do believe that churches can fulfill their God given role. How is that accomplished though? We've been conditioned our whole life to look at the church in the wrong way, which is what we are going to discuss today.

There is an awesome book by Michael Frost and Alan Hirsch entitled, *The Shaping of Things to Come,* in which they give their ideas of what the church should look like. I must admit, this book has rocked my world. While I don't agree with every single word they say, I do think they've hit the nail on the head. When I initially read this book, it was like I could finally see the church for the first time. We will discuss their ideas at various points through today's discussion.

Growing up I was always frustrated with church. To me it was comfortable and boring and held little interest. My comfort was only in knowing that when I had to go there each Sunday I could just coast–I wasn't going to be challenged in any way. The people that went to my church were mostly white, middle-class families like me and it was easy to do nothing. When I was able to leave that church at eighteen, I church-hopped for years and years–just hoping I would find a fun church to be a part of. I never found it because I was looking for the wrong things.

Does this sound familiar? By the way, I did not talk about "white-middle class families" to be racial or stereotype the church. However, it does bring up a point and the way in which I want to attack this issue.

"Birds of a feather flock together"–heard that saying before? It means people tend to hang out with people that are like them–their culture. Churches today tend to be dominated by the group I've already talked about–so why aren't the "other" groups represented in the church? The simple answer is that the church is not doing enough to reach them or they are hiding out in mega churches.

The reason small churches are closing their doors everyday and mega churches are doing so well is because they look good. Much of the growth though is transfer growth–people going from one church to another. People often go to these churches because they look good and it's easy to go to. No, this chapter is not going to go off on mega churches. Some mega churches are doing some very wonderful things and maybe your church is one of them.

Take a look at the mission-minded Christians of the early church. They met in people's homes and were a part of the community they were in. They gave to the poor and fellowshipped together *daily*. Paul and other apostles traveled between churches to encourage them in their faith, fellowship with them, and correct leaders.

That changed when Constantine made Christianity the official state church of Rome in 312 BC. Overnight the church went from periods of intense persecution to being the toast of the town. In a word, the church became *institutionalized*—and it's been that way ever since. Think about what you've seen in churches. How much variety have you seen between them? For the most part churches sing the same number of songs every week and listen to a pastor for about the same amount of time. Interestingly, that's true of most faiths in the Christian world.

What kind of people were in the early church? Tax collectors, former prostitutes, carpenters. . . . basically every kind of person, including many Romans. They were truly willing to accept anyone—so why can't we? A teacher once told me about how his church reacted when a very grungy looking homeless person once walked into his church to the front row and sat down right in the middle of the service. Let's face it, the majority of churches today would not readily accept this type of individual into their services. Why? Since when did we get to be too good for anyone else? We're not any more holy than that individual—Jesus showed us that in his earthly ministry.

We've only scratched the surface here, but this is already a lot to think about so I'm going to end with one more thought. No doubt this will spark some good discussions with your friends—I know it did with me. I want to end here with a short discussion of church unity. How many denominations can you count in the early church? As hard as I look, I still only count one. There were house churches in many major cities, but they were one people, serving one God, and helping each other with money and resources.

Now, it's important to note here that I am not calling for one world church. Some would say that would be the beginning of the end times. What I am asking is, can you imagine what would happen if churches put aside their petty arguments and worked together for the glory of God? The thought is too powerful to comprehend! There are examples of churches banding together for various outreach ministries all over the world. They've had great success because they have learned what is truly important in life. Why can't more churches band together in this way?

Questions:

1. How do you view church? What are some of the turnoffs? What positives are there?

2. Name some reasons you feel churches have become bogged down in "petty arguments"?

3. What events or changes do you think would have to take place before unification of the church could happen?

OPEN MOUTH, INSERT FOOT

HARD TALK: THE SENT JESUS

➡ JESUS ANSWERED AND SAID TO THEM, "THIS IS THE WORK OF GOD, THAT YOU BELIEVE IN HIM WHOM HE HAS SENT." JOHN 6:29 (NASB)

➡ JESUS SAID TO THEM, "IF GOD WERE YOUR FATHER, YOU WOULD LOVE ME, FOR I PROCEEDED FORTH AND HAVE COME FROM GOD, FOR I HAVE NOT EVEN COME ON MY OWN INITIATIVE, BUT HE SENT ME." JOHN 8:42 (NASB)

➡ "THIS IS ETERNAL LIFE, THAT THEY MAY KNOW YOU, THE ONLY TRUE GOD, AND JESUS CHRIST WHOM YOU HAVE SENT." JOHN 17:3 (NASB)

➡ SO JESUS SAID TO THEM AGAIN, " PEACE BE WITH YOU; AS THE FATHER HAS SENT ME, I ALSO SEND YOU." JOHN 20:21 (NASB)

Churches are not buildings but people—do you believe that? It is *you* and *me* that make up the church—not the building that we come to. It seems like churches today have the mistaken idea that they must attract people to them by building wonderful buildings, colorful stages, and great programs and ministries. Those can all be good things, but they are all meant to attract people *to* the church. What I want you to see today is that is not the way God intended it to be.

The greatest example of this that we have is Jesus himself. Jesus was *sent* to the earth to live a sinless life and fulfill His mission on the cross. While here, he hung out with completely sinful people and his disciples were more of the same. Take a minute and read through some of the verses I posted at the beginning of this chapter. Jesus was sent—plain and simple.

What does that mean for us? It means that we must go *to* the world, not wait for it to come to us. Church ministries are great—

even better if they are mission-minded ministries. That doesn't mean you ignore the internal structuring and needs of the church. Actually, I believe it means the ministries in the church reflect the needs within the church *and* the surrounding community.

What would it look like if the local church was actually in tune with the needs of the community? What if the local church was made up of a group of people that embraced anyone into their fellowship and went out into the community to be *with* the community? What that would look like!

You could say that one of the reasons Christianity grew was as a reaction against "religion." The Roman world embraced tolerance of virtually all religions at the time and was a polytheistic (many gods) culture. Most of these religions were structured, rigid, emotionless, and dead.

I believe you could argue that today much of the world is reacting against the "religion" of Christianity. The post-modern world is a world of no absolute truths–the only absolute truth being that there is no absolute truth. This kind of thought pattern has seeped into churches everywhere. It's important to understand that the world today doesn't want to be a part of the "religion" of Christianity. Am I saying there are no absolute truths? No, definitely not–but if we are to go out into the world, we need to understand what that world is like. Tomorrow we will get into this more.

Questions:

1. Take a few minutes to write about what your concept of the 'sent Jesus' is.

_____

_____

_____

2. What are your thoughts on absolute truth?

_____

_____

STEPHEN WINTERS

HARD TALK: A TALE OF TWO WORLDS

CHRISTIAN PICK-UP LINES:

- Nice Bible.
- I would like to pray with you.
- You know Jesus? Hey, me too!
- God told me to come talk to you.
- I know a church where we could go and talk.
- How about a hug, sister/brother?
- Do you need help carrying your Bible? It looks heavy.
- Christians don't shake hands; Christians gotta hug!
- Did it hurt when you fell from Heaven?
- What are your plans for tonight? Feel like a Bible study?
- I am here for you.
- The word says "Give drink to those who are thirsty, and feed the hungry"; how about dinner?
- You don't have an accountability partner? Me neither.
- You want to come over and watch the 10 commandments tonight?
- Is it a sin that you stole my heart?
- You know they say that you have never really dated, until you have dated a Christian!
- Would you happen to know a Christian man/woman that I could love with all my heart and wait on hand and foot?
- Nice bracelet. Who would Jesus date?
- Do you believe in Divine appointment?
- Have you ever tried praying at a drive in movie before?
- (For the ladies) Excuse me, I believe one of your ribs belongs to me.
- My friend told me to come and meet you, he said that you are a really nice person. I think you know him. Jesus, yeah, that's his name.

~unknown source

I believe much of Christianity today has now amounted to a tale of two worlds. On Sundays we go to church where we will find other people like us who want to do the church thing. We're comfortable there and it makes us feel good. We know what to expect and for many it's a simple game.

Then we leave and we go out into that "other world." Maybe we even get all the way through the whole day Sunday doing "God things," but come Monday morning we know that we are going to have to face the "real world." We decide we're going to put our game face on and we go about our other lives. Why do we have to live two separate lives? Why can't our Christian world and our real world be the same world?

I inserted the Christian pick up lines again as a humorous way to illustrate what I'm talking about. Pick up lines are something usually associated with the "secular" world right? Well, I found a way to mold the two together! Okay. . . . so obviously I'm kidding around, but do you get what I'm driving at here?

My entire life I've been taught to stay out of the secular world. If I keep the company of those of the world, I'll definitely be corrupted by them and there is no way I'll be able to keep my faith. Are we really that weak? I am not saying to only have non-Christian friends–honestly I think we should have both. Again, look at who Jesus surrounded Himself with.

This may come as a shock to you–because it certainly was a shock to me–but we are not any better than anyone else on this earth. Christians tend to think of themselves as above the world because we've found Christ and they haven't. This is a sad reality in the church and I'm as guilty as anyone of thinking that way. Jesus, the ultimate human, was a servant in everything He did. He even washed the disciple's feet!

Instead of thinking that we are better than the world, we should have a burden for reaching the world. That means engaging the world where they are and becoming a part of their lives. Does that mean you change your values or standards?

This will probably come as a revelation, like many things

we've talked about, but God is everywhere, not just at church. Church is not just a building—it's a group of people. Church is not just on Sunday; it's a fellowshipping community of brothers and sisters in Christ. It seems like Christians believe God only dwells in a church building and when we leave we've left the presence of God. God's presence should never leave us as we go throughout our week.

Youth groups today are often social clubs meant to keep youth away from the "corrupting influences of society." While I think there is serious value in all of that, there is great danger in youth being so sheltered from the world that they are ignorant to it all. Why? When those youth leave the church and face the real world, it's a world they know little about and don't know how to inter-act in. Their faith is shallow and a high percentage of them leave church.

It seems like we are taught a lot about how to act in the church and very little about how to interact in the world beyond the church doors. Who do we love? What type of friends should we keep? What do we actually *do* out *there?* Ever asked these questions?

Here's another good one—why is it that Christians are often stereotyped as hypocrites? Is that even a stereotype? I believe that answer has a lot to do with the way we separate our worlds. I was always taught to be "in the world, but not of the world." I believe that's a great statement, but what we've done with it is another story. Let's take a quick look at a few verses that have been misused in the church:

➡ "AND DO NOT BE CONFORMED TO THIS WORLD, BUT BE TRANSFORMED BY THE RENEWING OF YOUR MIND, SO THAT YOU MAY PROVE WHAT THE WILL OF GOD IS, THAT WHICH IS GOOD AND ACCEPTABLE AND PERFECT." (ROMANS 12:2 NASB)

➡ "DO NOT LOVE THE WORLD NOR THE THINGS IN THE WORLD. IF ANYONE LOVES THE WORLD, THE LOVE OF THE FATHER IS NOT IN HIM. FOR ALL THAT IS IN THE WORLD, THE LUST OF

THE FLESH AND THE LUST OF THE EYES AND THE BOASTFUL PRIDE OF LIFE, IS NOT FROM THE FATHER, BUT IS FROM THE WORLD." (1 JOHN 2:15–16 NASB)

➡"IF YOU WERE OF THE WORLD, THE WORLD WOULD LOVE ITS OWN; BUT BECAUSE YOU ARE NOT OF THE WORLD, BUT I CHOSE YOU OUT OF THE WORLD, BECAUSE OF THIS THE WORLD HATES YOU." (JOHN 15:19 NASB)

Where in these passages does it say we are to create an exclusive Christian club at church where many feel unworthy and unwelcome? Where does it say to keep our youth so sheltered that their faith is weak? Where does it say to ignore the needs of the community? Where does it say to stay locked up in our lives and forget Christ's command found in Matthew 28:19: "Go therefore and make disciples of all the nations, baptizing them in the name of the Father and the Son and the Holy Spirit." *(NASB)* The verses above are all about not being conformed to the things we know we shouldn't.

Now, some of you might point out that I did a whole section earlier in this book on not being in a hurry to lose our innocence. There is a big difference in being in a hurry to lose our innocence and being salt and light to the world around us. One knowingly embraces sin; the other is an example *amongst* the sin of Christ. Does that make sense to you? Talk with someone about it until it does make sense to you because it is a very important point.

People say, "Well, why do you want to put temptation in your life?" No offense, but that is a personal issue—one that I've wrestled with a lot. I think I finally understand the answer to this argument and it's found in I Corinthians 10:13, "No temptation has overtaken you but such as is common to man; and God is faithful, who will not allow you to be tempted beyond what you are able, but with the temptation will provide the way of escape also, so that you will be able to endure it." *(NASB)* Classically, Christians have wrongly pointed to this verse to say that God will never put anything in your life that you can't handle. The real context for this verse is what we are talking about right now.

Yes, you should have Christian friends and Christian fellowship. These two things are incredibly important to you as I've discussed before. But why can't you and your Christian friends go *into* the world as Christ commands? I used to think that missions was all about going to Africa and "saving" the villagers. That's wonderful for those who have answered that call because the need is great, but I've come to realize that missions is all about your own backyard. Perhaps the greatest mission field you will find is your community. There are people struggling all around you and you can reach out to them. The homeless person downtown, the single mom next door who needs help babysitting her four year old son, the Vietnam veteran across the street—they are all around you.

I've got two words for you that rocked my world—culturally relevant. To me part of what makes a "good church" is one that is ministering to the needs of their community *and* a church that understands that the culture around them is changing all the time. How can we minister to the needs of our communities if we don't know anything about it?

To borrow a line from the movie *Napoleon Dynamite,* "bow-hunting skills, knumchuck skills, computer hacking skills . . ." This movie is essentially about nothing, but it's funny and this line hits upon a wonderful truth. God has given each of you some kind of talent. Maybe you are incredibly good at sports. Perhaps you are an awesome skateboarder. Perhaps you are a computer geek. Maybe you're all of the above. Whatever your skills are, there is probably some type of sub-culture in your community where you could use those hobbies and talents to become a part of a group. They aren't going to come to you—you have to go to them. When you do become a part of a group, don't think that you have to "save" them your first day. First, we don't do the saving, that is the role of the Holy Spirit. Second, it may take years of interacting in these groups before they ever ask you about your faith or an opportunity presents itself. If one person comes to know the joy you have in Christ through that—wouldn't it be worth it?

OPEN MOUTH, INSERT FOOT

As a Christian, I was taught to stay out of the world and I've come to realize I was arrogant to think this way. This type of thinking drives people away from the church. All the different sects of the Christian faith have a corner on the truth so they can't all be right–right? It's easy to see why a non-Christian would look at that arrogance and division and not want to bother with it.

If you have not yet seen the movie "End of the Spear," I would suggest doing so as soon as possible. It's sad that it didn't do better in the theatres because it is a fantastic movie. The concept of making the gospel culturally relevant is rammed home by five lines in the movie. If you ever see me speak in person on this subject, there is a good chance I'll be showing that clip. Go see the movie and you'll completely understand what I'm talking about–you can't miss it.

Today I'm going to leave you with a few questions. Some of them have already been asked in this chapter, some are new. All of them deserve your thought. Be honest with yourself and don't be afraid to have some good discussions with others about them.

Questions:

1. What are your thoughts on the subject of truth?

_____

2. Who are we apart from Sunday?

_____

3. How do we interact with the world? What is our role?

_____

4. What is a church? What is its role? What is a church building to you?

_____

5. Does a church have to have a purpose?

_____

6. To be a "good" Christian—do you have to be "saving" people?

_____

7. How can we be separate from the world? What does it look like or should we even be separate at all?

_____

_____

8. What if churches worked together? What if churches were more aware of the culture around them and less afraid of it? What would our world look like?

_____

9. What are some ways you can embrace the culture of your community?

_____

_____

ⓐ Journal:

_____

_____

_____

_____

_____

_____

_____

_____

_____

_____

_____

_____

SHARING YOUR FAITH

Most of us fear the ridicule of sharing our faith so it's something that we tend to put off till later. "I'll get to it eventually," most of us say. "I'm just busy right now." "I'll wait till I know more because I'm not an expert." This thinking is dangerous!

SHARING YOUR FAITH: GOD'S WORD AND UNITY

➡ "THE HUMBLEST INDIVIDUAL EXERTS SOME INFLUENCE, EI-
THER FOR GOOD OR EVIL, UPON OTHERS."
~HENRY WARD BEECHER

➡ "I AM BUT A FOREIGNER HERE ON EARTH; I NEED THE GUID-
ANCE OF YOUR COMMANDS. DON'T HIDE THEM FROM ME!"
~PSALMS 119:19

We are aliens on this earth! God didn't put us here to stay, but to do His work and move on. I've heard these sentiments all my life but I never really applied them. This seemed as good of a place for me to spend eternity as any. Boy was I wrong! We can't imagine what is in store for us in heaven, as the following passages agree with:

Colossians 1:5: You do this because you are looking forward to the joys of heaven-as you have been ever since you first heard the truth of the Good News.

Hebrews 11:16: But they were looking for a better place, a heavenly homeland. That is why God is not ashamed to be called their god, for he has prepared a heavenly city for them.

Revelations 21:10—27: So he took me in spirit to a great, high mountain, and he showed me the holy city, Jerusalem, descending out of heaven from God. It was filled with the glory of God and sparkled like a precious gem, crystal clear like jasper.

How awesome it will be when we get there. Until then though we have a job to do here on this earth. Matthew 28: 18–20:

Jesus came and told his disciples, "I have been given complete authority in heaven and on earth. Therefore, go and make disciples of all the nations, baptizing them in the name of the Father and the Son and the Holy Spirit. Teach these new disciples to obey all the commands I have given you. And be sure of this: I am with you always, even to the end of the age."

Questions:

1. Name some reasons you feel churches have become bogged down in "petty arguments"?

_____

_____

_____

2. What events or changes do you think would have to take place before unification of the church could happen?

_____

_____

_____

OPEN MOUTH, INSERT FOOT

SHARING YOUR FAITH: THE CHOICE

➡ "EVERY CHOICE MOVES US CLOSER TO OR FARTHER AWAY FROM SOMETHING. WHERE ARE YOUR CHOICES TAKING YOUR LIFE? WHAT DO YOUR BEHAVIORS DEMONSTRATE THAT YOU ARE SAYING YES OR NO TO IN LIFE?"

~ERIC ALLENBAUGH

➡ "TO HAVE A CHOICE TO MAKE AND TO NOT MAKE IT, IS A CHOICE IN ITSELF."

~UNKNOWN AUTHOR

It seems today there's a "Christian" band for every type of music out there. Allow me to give a little plug to the words of a couple of songs that are among my favorites. The songs are off of DC Talk's "Jesus Freak" CD. All the words to the songs are not given; just the lines that I'd like you to key into.

JESUS FREAK

What will people think when they hear that I'm
a Jesus freak
What will people do when they find out it's true
I don't really care if they label me a Jesus freak
There ain't no disguising the truth
People say I'm strange, does it make me a stranger,
That my best friend was born in a manger

IN THE LIGHT

I keep trying to find a life, on my own, apart from you
I am the king of excuses, I've got one for every selfish
thing I do
What's going on inside of me, I despise my own behavior
This only serves to confirm my suspicions, That I'm still in
need of a savior
I wanna be in the Light, as you are in the Light
I wanna shine like the stars in the Heavens
Oh, Lord be my Light and be my salvation
Cause all I want is to be in the Light

These songs remind me of exactly where I should always be in my walk with God. I shouldn't care how I'm labeled, but I should be making strides every day towards always living and focusing on being "in the Light." To me these songs exemplify the challenge of witnessing to others that God has set before us.

Why do you think it is that we do so little when God so explicitly tells us why we have been put here? Sometimes I think it is because we are not challenged enough. We go to school each day and are generally "good" people and come home with no one being the wiser as to who we really are. What a meaningless existence! We might not realize it now, but we will someday meet the Lord and He will ask us what we did with our lives. Do you want to tell Him you did nothing?

I wonder how we would respond if suddenly our country became communist overnight. Freedom would be gone in an instant and we may wonder where our next meal was coming from. Armed soldiers would roam the hallways of our schools waiting for anyone to get out of line. I wonder if we would still attend church secretly or let all the world know that we were Christians. How would you respond?

When it comes down to a decision of dying for our faith or living in sin, I wouldn't be surprised if the majority of us would die for our faith. We would be Simon of Cyrene carrying Christ's cross up to the hill. We'd even carry our own cross up that hill. We would stand in front of a firing squad and shout our faith for all to hear until the firing of the rifles silenced us. I think for most of us our faith is real enough that many would do this for Jesus.

Fortunately, or unfortunately, depending on how you look at it, our world is not like that. Life and death and what comes in-between is not so clear for us. It would be easier to die for our faith than to give up the daily control we crave. We know what we are supposed to do, yet we don't do it for fear of the consequences. Being labeled a "Jesus freak" at school would tarnish our reputation in the eyes of the world. Taking a chance and witnessing to someone might damage our popularity points. We'd rather live a life of sin than be "falsely accused."

What I'd like to convince you of is that everything in life is about choices and the choice between life and death is one of them. The Bible says that Jesus will come back as a thief in the night. Of course you know that as long as you've truly accepted Jesus Christ as your Savior you have nothing to worry about in respect to your salvation and your place in heaven.

However, I give you this question to think about: What about everyone else? What about that guy or girl you were supposed to witness to when God gave you the opportunity the other day and you missed it? What if they die tomorrow and go to hell? Sobering to think about, isn't it? If you love them you will let nothing, including your own fears, get in the way of sharing the good news. Remember, love is a choice, an action.

I'd be the first one to tell you that I'm no model citizen when it comes to witnessing. The important thing is realizing it and doing something about it. To not do something about it at this point would be the same as a lung cancer patient realizing that smoking cigarettes since he was twelve has led him to the point he is at and he still goes home and smokes two packs a day.

James 1:23–24 states it this way: "For if anyone is a hearer of the word and not a doer, he is like a man who looks at his natural face in a mirror; for once he has looked at himself and gone away, he has immediately forgotten what kind of person he was." *(NASB)*

Questions:

1. What is your biggest fear in witnessing?

2. What are some smaller steps you could take in order to conquer your biggest fear?

_____

_____

_____

_____

Journal:

_____

_____

_____

_____

_____

_____

_____

_____

_____

_____

_____

_____

_____

_____

_____

_____

_____

_____

SHARING YOUR FAITH: REACTIONS

➡ "WHAT YOU DO SPEAKS SO LOUD THAT I CANNOT HEAR WHAT YOU SAY."

~RALPH WALDO EMERSON

➡ "OF TWO EVILS, CHOOSE NEITHER."

~CHARLES HADDON SPURGEON

➡ "NOTHING WOULD BE DONE AT ALL IF ONE WAITED UNTIL ONE COULD DO IT SO WELL THAT NO ONE COULD FIND FAULT WITH IT."

~CARDINAL J. NEWMAN

➡ "IF THERE WAS NOTHING WRONG IN THE WORLD THERE WOULDN'T BE ANYTHING FOR US TO DO."

~GEORGE BERNARD SHAW

I think before we can expect to conquer the world we must conquer our own fears and inadequacies. I don't know about you but the scariest thing for me about witnessing is how the other person will react. I'd kind of relate it to the fear of asking someone out or showing interest in someone. I mean, what if they laugh at me? Will others around us laugh at me too? How do I know when it's the right time to witness? The answer? All the time! Your whole life should be an example, a stand, a billboard, a sign, a light in the darkness. Perhaps a good rule of thumb is if we are questioning whether the moment is the right time—then it is the right time!

The Bible tells us that people can react in one of five ways:

They could be afraid of change: Luke 8:37
They could laugh at you: Luke 8: 51–53
They could practice conditional following: Luke 9: 57–62
They could test Jesus: Luke 10: 25
They could unconditionally follow Jesus: Luke 5: 27–28

The first four reactions might seem negative initially—but that should not really be your concern. They may react that way, but no matter what, you've given them at least one opportunity to choose Jesus and you may have planted a growing seed that is going to lead them to Jesus soon.

What I'd like to convince you of is that you have absolutely no control as to which way a person will react to what you have to say. You have control as to how you witness (tone, inflections, style) and your methods will always have room for improvement, but ultimately the choice lies in the mind of the other person and God. News flash: God knew exactly who you would witness to and how they would react before you were even born. If God knows all these things, don't you think we could put our petty fears aside and take steps of faith? Take comfort in this—God knows what He's doing! God gives each of us many opportunities, sometimes every day, and yet we still don't act on them. This has to change!

The world today is skeptical of Christians. People say there are no absolute truths—things agreed upon as truths in the past are no longer agreed on. Witnessing is best done through relationships. By that I mean they need to *see* Christ in you before they are ever going to really listen to what you have to say. Does that mean spur of the moment witnessing to absolute strangers won't happen? No, there is still a time and a place for that. What I am saying is you need to first *live* your faith so your friends can see it in you and then be willing to step to the plate and have a conversation about Christ with them. Be honest—be open—and don't be afraid to not have the right answers. God will give you the words and you can rely on the help of Christian friends and leaders to help you find the answers when you don't know.

Questions:

1. Read each of the passages above that deal with the five ways a person could react. Which one of these reactions scares you the most and what is one way you can think of to overcome your fear?

_____

2. Think of the last time you tried to witness to someone. In what way (if any) did they reject it? (Describe)

_____

3. Has that negative experience kept you from trying to witness again?

_____

⊛ Journal:

_____

STEPHEN WINTERS

SHARING YOUR FAITH: MOTIVATION

"Jesus replied, 'You must love the Lord your God with all your heart, all your soul, and all your mind. This is the first and greatest commandment. A second is equally important: Love your neighbor as yourself. All the other commandments and all the demands of the prophet are based on these two commandments.'" Matthew 22:37–40

At some point in your life you're going to have to ask yourself, "What is my motivation in life?" Is it money, power, sex, or drugs? Maybe it's being the most popular or something simple like making it through high school or college without being singled out for your faith. Maybe it's your career or your future marriage. What we need to understand now is that all these things will work themselves out. God has been doing His job very well for all of time and He's not going to stop now. He put us on this earth to do one thing: glorify Him in everything we do! We do this through the greatest commandment of loving God with everything we have. Re-read the verse above and you'll see what I'm saying. He's given us the means, the will, and the way; it's up to us to act on it.

Ultimately, living a good life is not enough. Eventually we must step out of our comfort zone and be willing to talk about our faith. Start small though–witnessing will come naturally. Eventually your comfort zone will grow so big that you have no problem talking to anyone about your faith. Don't believe me? Try it and see what happens. Who knows, you might just be the next Billy Graham!

Questions:

1. What are your motivations in life?

_____

_____

_____

2. Who is one person you know that needs to hear the gospel?

_____

3. Are you willing to do what the Lord asks of you concerning this person?

_____

_____

_____

Journal:

_____

_____

_____

_____

_____

_____

_____

_____

_____

_____

_____

_____

_____

_____

_____

SHARING YOUR FAITH: BE REAL!

➡ "WE ARE LIKE CHAMELEONS; WE TAKE OUR HUE AND THE COLOR OF OUR MORAL CHARACTER, FROM THOSE WHO ARE AROUND US."

~JOHN LOCKE

Do you know what could be your best tool in sharing your faith? Being real! The biggest turnoff to the world about Christians is hypocrisy. No one likes a hypocrite, yet our churches are filled with them. We all go to church on Sundays—saying and doing the "right" things and the rest of our weeks are filled with a mediocre lifestyle that is a slap in the face to everything that God is trying to teach us. Non-Christians are tired of seeing Christians who say one thing and do another. They can easily see through our fake fronts.

We must learn to LIVE our faith! People who are truly passionate about something are contagious! You want to learn to share your faith? First learn to be real! Be real about who you are; be real about your faith; be real about growing in Him! Believe me people—Christians and non-Christians alike—will want to know what it is you have!

Why do (or did) you go to youth group? Because it was fun? Because you like the music? Perhaps you like being able to see that really cute person of the opposite sex in a setting our parents would allow. Many youth groups today are little more than glorified social clubs filled with mediocre posers. Tough words? You bet! I point the finger at myself as well since my biggest reason for going to groups was to be entertained.

We need to make groups more about God and less about looking attractive. Attractiveness to non-Christians comes in being real! Believe it!

I would love to see Christian youth become real, impactful people. Our motivations for our words would stem from honesty and commitment to Him and each other rather than just saying what we feel we are supposed to say. This is where true growth begins! We have to take an honest look at ourselves. The way to grow is not to say the right things but to know what our faults are and work on them.

Do these sound like strange words to you? I bet they do! No doubt if a whole youth group decided to adopt this philosophy the level of Christianity might appear to weaken. Someone might swear or maybe sex would be discussed more openly. I'll tell you what though; you'd certainly know Christ was there! What an absolutely *attractive* place that would be! Non-Christians would come and feel welcome. People would be more open about sharing who they really are. Intimacy among small groups would foster growth at the heart of issues. A sense of true camaraderie would be evident and lives would be eternally changed! People wouldn't be distracted—wouldn't you want to come to a place like that? I know I would!

What I want you to see is that these are the kinds of people we must be. True growth begins with being real about who we are and where we're going. God will honor you for it and everyone—especially your non-Christian friends—will take notice!

So it's easy for me to tell you "be real" and leave it at that, but no doubt some of you could be asking me what that means. I don't have any magic answer on the "do's" and "don'ts" of being real people, but I can give you some suggestions. Don't get caught up in the world's version of everyday conversation. Gossip has no place in your world. Encourage your friends to be affectionate people in a Christ-like way and model that for the other kids in your youth group. Read your Bible and practice learning to talk about God by having conversations about Him and what He is doing in your life with your Christian friends. Don't be afraid to initiate a community service project for the homeless in your area with the people in your youth group. These are just a few of the ways I believe we can learn to be more real in our Christian walk. What other ways can you think of?

Questions:

1. What does the word "real" mean to you in your own life?

_____

....

_____

2. What are some ways you can get your youth group involved in your local community?

....

_____

....

Journal:

_____

....

_____

....

_____

....

_____

....

_____

....

_____

....

_____

....

_____

....

....

_____

_____

....

SHARING YOUR FAITH: THE JOY OF OPTIMISM!

➡ "AMONG THOSE WHOM I LIKE OR ADMIRE, I CAN FIND NO
COMMON DENOMINATOR, BUT AMONG THOSE WHOM I LOVE,
I CAN: ALL OF THEM MAKE ME LAUGH. "

~W. H. AUDEN

Yesterday we discussed the concept of being real in our walk with God. Today I want to discuss the joy that optimism can bring. I look at the world around me and frankly it's not an attractive place. Globally, I see wars dividing nations, diseases running rampant, governments abusing powers and the list goes on. Within America we see our individualistic attitudes at an all-time high, the family unit breaking down, gay marriages becoming legal, people murdered in the streets, and churches closing their doors daily.

Optimism. What a fantastic word! Optimistic people are fun to be around. They tend to be upbeat and outgoing and usually have infectious personalities. On the other hand, pessimistic people "see the cup as being only half-full" and are difficult to be around. To them everything that can go wrong, will go wrong. Think of someone you know that's pessimistic. Am I right?

I consider myself to be an optimistic realist. I want to be that upbeat person that people want to be around. Yet I try to balance that with the reality of the nasty world around me. The world focuses on negativity. Don't believe me? Turn on the average newscast and listen for five minutes. How many positive things do you hear being discussed? Usually very little, if any at all.

So if reality is that the world is a bad place, then why should we choose to be optimistic? The answer is easy and wonderful! Because we're on the winning side and we know the promises of tomorrow! If you are a Christian, you will be in God's kingdom, a place where sin will never be. Everything that's happening in the world is as it should be. Since the fall of man in the Garden of Eden, the world was plunged into sin. It is an inescapable part of our existence. In fact, the world will only get worse over time as we

STEPHEN WINTERS

move towards the return of Christ; the Bible promises us this. That is not a reason to give up–it's the fuel to push us on! We should be so excited about the promises we have in Christ that we can't help but share it with others! We've already got the conclusion–now let's write the story that God intended!

Questions:

1. Think of the most optimistic person you know. What makes that person attractive to be around?

_____

_____

_____

Journal:

_____

_____

_____

_____

_____

_____

_____

_____

_____

_____

_____

A DEEPER LOOK

I am no expert, nor do I claim to be one. The following chapter is a mid-level discussion of some topics that are of great interest to me. The purpose of this chapter is to let you know what I've learned on this subject and to encourage you to search these subjects out even more. I'll try to point you in the right direction by giving you some books you can look at (suggested reading with a "ROTF" means a recommendation of trusted friend).

A DEEPER LOOK: TEMPTATIONS

It was the first time I'd gone with my youth group to Wednesday at the beach for surfing and some fun. It was just after lunch and we stepped onto the hot sand and started toward the water. I carried a boogey board and a small backpack. There were ten of us and our leader, Jim. I was really excited!

I looked straight ahead as I walked, concentrating on picking up my feet as quickly as I could—the sand was hot!!! We finally got there and I threw my stuff down, laid my towel down and lay down on top of it. Moving over on my side, I looked around. Wow! There were bikinis everywhere I turned. I realized I was staring at one woman and she gave me a smile. I looked away, uncomfortable. I mean, I wasn't supposed to be looking, right?

I turned back around to our group and could see the five girls with us were all in various stages of taking off their clothes and putting on sunscreen. I tried to concentrate on their faces when they spoke—that was hard because I was very shy and eye contact was difficult. But where else could I look? I wished I was like the other guys there who seemed as calm as ever—I wondered what the secret was. This was going to be a long afternoon. . . .

It is very difficult to stay away from sexual temptation; sex is everywhere. There will probably be very few times in your life when sexual temptation is not there. So what do you do? Are there any answers?

Ladies, indulge me a moment by letting me share these more obvious pieces of advice with the guys: Stay away from pornographic material! Sounds obvious, but pornography will lead you places that are hard to come back from. Also, when you see that hot girl walking by, don't allow yourself a second look and don't allow your mind to dwell on it. If you do, it's going to be like giving a rocket the fuel it needs to take off and then trying to hold it down with your hands. Nearly impossible! By the way, if you think that curiosity about pornography and other things is something you will grow out of, don't count on it. I know married men who still struggle intensely with it. Find a way to overcome this addiction now . . .

I loved going to the beach, but around the end of high school I realized that my reasons for going to the beach had changed from love of the sand and water to what kind of babes I might see. I decided to limit my trips to the beach and found other activities to occupy my time.

When you're at the movies and a love scene is being played out, don't be afraid to look away for a few seconds. You'd be surprised how short they can be. When you allow yourself to see them, it can be devastating to your mind later. Most of you say this is easier said than done. Believe me, I know what you're saying! Just try it once and see how much satisfaction it takes out of your movie experience. I bet it's not much and you might enjoy that movie more free from guilt!

If you're feeling brave, make a commitment to screen every movie before you go to see it. There are some very good websites out there that measure and rate movies against Christian standards—a simple internet search will guide you to these sites. Determine what your temptation is. Some people struggle with language, some with violence, while others struggle with sex and sensuality. You might ask why I separate sex and sensuality. While many movies leave out actual sex or nudity, they still contain a lot of sensuality. A sensually dressed woman can be just as dangerous for our thought life. Lusting after someone is demeaning because it is treating them like an object instead of a person. Lust is an exercise of selfishness and God calls us to be selfless, not selfish.

I'm reminded of a line from a recent movie, "*Win a Date With Tad Hamilton.*" A protective friend yells out to his friend who has won a date with the famous Tad Hamilton, "Guard your carnal treasure!" How wise that line is! I wish the women of our society today would buy into that—especially Christian women.

Ladies, for us guys there's nothing more tempting than an alluringly dressed girl walking by. It's not that hard to get a guy to give you a second look. Yet, you've been told your entire life that you must dress "sexy" to be noticed. Where does God say that? Whoever came up with that myth needs a reality check. There's nothing more beautiful than a girl dressed in the humility and grace of God.

JOSHUA HARRIS SAYS IT THIS WAY,

"If you want godly men to respect and cherish you as a woman, refuse to buy in to our culture's obsession with being physically beautiful and sexually alluring. This is an attitude that springs from the motives of your heart and extends to the way you dress and act around men. Is your wardrobe an expression of your love for God? What's your motive? Have you ever asked your father or another Christian woman to honestly evaluate your clothing? Are you willing to sacrifice fashion to be obedient to God? In Scripture, Peter tells Christian women that their beauty should be that of their inner selves——'the unfading beauty of a gentle and quiet spirit, which is of great worth in God's sight" (I Peter 3:4)." **Boy Meets Girl: Say Hello to Courtship**

OPEN MOUTH, INSERT FOOT

His wife, Shannon, adds, "There's a big difference between dressing attractively and dressing to attract."

For you guys out there, we're not off the hook that easily. We must commit to not giving the second look. Instead of lusting after the opposite sex we should put our energies into learning how to love the opposite sex as sisters in Christ by protecting, loving, encouraging and respecting them.

How do you not give that second look? Well, there are different methods and you need to find what works for you. Some people suggest training your mind to think about something else when you see something alluring. So the next time your mind subconsciously thinks of that again, instead of focusing on the alluring sight. For me, it has been very helpful to change how I view girls. Instead of every time I meet a girl thinking "could this be a girl I'm going to date?" I try to view each girl as a sister in Christ. I have to say that it has been absolutely liberating learning to love my sisters in Christ!

Once you start down any road of sin, it is very difficult to return. To this day I still deal with many of the temptations that I grew up trying to confront. I deal with keeping my speech free from four-letter words, my attitude where it should be, and my thoughts in the right place. The list of things Satan can tempt us with is endless.

Ultimately everything in life comes down to choices; this is fundamental to our existence. Think it through and you'll realize everything in your life involves choices. Hopefully you've chosen to accept Jesus Christ as your Savior and are allowing Him to dictate your life.

Now it's time for you to choose to resist Satan's attempts on you. It's not easy. At some point you will fail. Whenever we go on our own strength we are guaranteed to fail–our flesh is weak. Lucky for us we know a God that allows us to repent of our sins so that He may forgive us of those sins.

Professional athletes will tell you that part of the reason they got where they are today is because of practice and past failures.

Learning from their mistakes helped them put together a better game plan for the next time. It's the same way in our lives. The practice that we need to succeed is hiding God's Word in our hearts so when Satan challenges us we have what we need to combat him. Something I'd like to convince you of before we're through is how important a strong relationship with the Lord is in resisting Satan. Picture this for a moment:

You are standing on a bridge made of vines over a deep canyon. God is in front of you beckoning you to Him while Satan is behind cutting as many vines as he can. The more you obey God, read His Word, and are in constant prayer with Him, the more vines that appear on your bridge. The more vines there are, the less the bridge sways, and the easier it is to make progress towards the ultimate relationship with Him. The less you do these things, the weaker your bridge becomes until you are eventually attempting a tight rope act.

We have no hope of resisting Satan unless we are in constant communion with God. Something I've started doing when I pray is holding my hands together—for some reason this helps me to concentrate a lot more. Some people like to get on their knees when they pray or go in a dark place. My sister likes to get out in nature. What is it for you? Do you know?

One of the most important things you can do in life is to get an accountability partner. An accountability partner should be of the same sex because that person will better understand what you're going through. Speak to this person several times a week, every day if possible. Lifting each other up in the spirit of Christ is one of the best ways to deny Satan his plans for you.

ECCLESIASTES 4: 712 SAYS:

"I observed yet another example of meaninglessness in our world. This is the case of a man who is alone, without a child or a brother, yet who works hard to gain as much wealth as he can. But then he asks himself, "Who am I working for? Why am I giving up so much pleasure now?" It is all so meaningless and depressing. Two people can accomplish more than twice as much as one; they get a better return for their labor. If one person falls, the other can reach out and help. But people who are alone when they fall are in real trouble. And on a cold night, two under the same blanket can gain warmth from each other. But how can one be warm alone? A person standing alone can be attacked and defeated, but two can stand back-to-back and conquer. Three are even better, for a triple-braided cord is not easily broken."

I want to finish off with this thought: any moral compromises we make now hurt our future spouse and our future marriage. Imagine having to tell your serious girlfriend or boyfriend, perhaps future spouse, everything you've done—or are doing now. Maybe we should try to keep that in mind as we interact with our partners. Many times we're convinced that who we are with is "the one." I've been there—it's how I lost my virginity. Let me tell you something—if the person you are with is someone you should be with, they will respect the moral standards you set for yourself and know you are worth waiting for!

I challenge you to read through the Songs of Solomon in your spare time. It is one of the greatest love stories you will ever hear and it's found in the Bible! Bet you didn't think you'd find that kind of stuff in the Bible! Who do you think gave us our strong sexual drives? Although sometimes it may seem like it's Satan, it's God who gives us our sex drive. As hard as it is to stay sexually pure, we should not be cursing God for our sex drive, but thanking Him that he gave us something so wonderful to look forward to!

➡"IT IS EASIER TO STAY OUT THAN GET OUT."

~MARK TWAIN

➡"I CAN RESIST EVERYTHING EXCEPT TEMPTATION."

~OSCAR WILDE

➡"WE USUALLY KNOW WHAT WE CAN DO, BUT TEMPTATION SHOWS US WHO WE ARE."

~THOMAS KEMPIS

STEPHEN WINTERS

➡ "EVERY MOMENT OF RESISTANCE TO TEMPTATION IS A VICTORY."

~FREDERICK FABER

SUGGESTED READING FOR A DEEPER LOOK INTO THIS SUBJECT:

Boy Meets Girl: Say Hello To Courtship by Joshua Harris

Every-Young Woman's Battle: Guarding Your Mind, Heart, and Soul in a Sex-Saturated World by Shannon Etheridge (ROTF)

Sex and the Single Guy: Winning Your Battle for Purity by Joseph Knable (ROTF)

Questions:

1. Do you have any standards that you go by in judging a movie before you see it? If not, will you prayerfully consider adopting some standards?

_____

_____

_____

2. How does praying affect your moral standards?

_____

_____

_____

3. Are you "dressing attractively" or "dressing to attract?" Will you commit to dressing the way God would want: "in the humility and grace of God?"

_____

_____

_____

OPEN MOUTH, INSERT FOOT

4. Will you pray now for strength to see those of the opposite sex as brothers and sisters in Christ? _____

Journal:

_____
_____
_____
_____
_____
_____
_____
_____
_____
_____
_____
_____
_____
_____
_____
_____
_____
_____
_____
_____
_____
_____
_____
_____

STEPHEN WINTERS

A DEEPER LOOK: WE'RE ENGAGED – PRACTICALLY THE SAME AS BEING MARRIED. . . . ISN'T IT?

"Huh?" I asked groggily. We'd just finished watching a movie. It was very late and I wasn't very coherent; I always fell asleep watching movies.

"I said you can just sleep here tonight if you want," she answered, as she untangled herself from my legs and got off the couch. "I don't want you to crash going home."

"Oh . . . ummm. . . . I don't think I should." I didn't like her getting up—I missed her already. I thought about it for a minute. I didn't really want to go home anyway, and it was only one night. I could just sleep on the couch. "Umm . . . on second thought, you're probably right. . . ."

We're engaged–practically the same as being married–isn't it? No! Despite what we've been conditioned to believe, this is a lie. Most of us take it–hook, line, and sinker! Why is it that Christians are not above this? Why do we have similar divorce rates? Why is it that we can so easily end up living together and/or being sexually active? We are called to be salt and light to the world, yet the world sees few lights. We blend in because we don't want to be different, and completely miss the point of our existence.

We were put on this earth for one reason–to glorify God in all that we do. The Bible is very clear about this. God did not have to let us exist. We should feel honored just to be alive. With that in mind, why do we care about things like popularity? Do you think popularity in your life now will mean anything to you in five years?

That may be an unfair thing to ask you right now because it's hard to see popularity for what it really is. If I had a dollar for every time I've heard someone look back on their past and wish they hadn't wasted their time trying to be popular, I'd be a rich man!

The same can be said for how we live our "love" lives before marriage. How are we glorifying Him by living together, or by having pre-marital sex? The world will tell you that it's a great idea to live together before you get married. After all, you want to make sure you are compatible right? Wrong again! Bad idea! There are a multitude of reasons why it's not a good idea:

- We say we trust Him to find us the right person, yet we want to live with them just to be sure He didn't screw it up? How is that trusting God?
- These actions aren't glorifying God.
- We cause other Christians to stumble.
- It is obedient to God – He calls us to leave or families for a husband or wife.

The same can be said for pre-marital sex activities. Let me tell you there are a whole lot of things you can do besides actual intercourse that are just as displeasing to Him. I can tell you how easy it is to get sucked into the lie that it's all okay because we're getting married. We never start out with that end in mind. It's a process. We are very good at rationalizing every action until eventually it's all okay with us. If you get anything else out of this week, remember this: Every excuse you make is an opportunity to fail!

Until the pastor says, "I now pronounce you husband and wife," there is little that you should allow yourself to be doing. How you define "little" is something that is between you and God. The time to figure that out is *before* you are in a relationship. Once you've decided what this will be, let me encourage you to stick to it with every fiber of your being. The danger comes in compromising. Compromise comes easiest when we are not in the Word and are not utilizing good accountability. Scripture and a solid accountability partner will more easily point out something as a compromise, so we don't lull ourselves into pretending it's logical. They are both like a light of truth that will shine a light on all the "logic" that could lead you towards sin.

A word of warning that I'd like to finish with is this: when you are in a relationship, don't allow yourself to become isolated from your family and friends. You are so much more prone to failure when your world only revolves around one person while in the dating/engagement phase and you have no voice of common sense from your friends/family to point out when you're rationalizing/compromising. If your relationship is strong enough, it can stand some time apart.

SUGGESTED READING FOR A DEEPER LOOK INTO THIS SUBJECT:
> *Why Wait?* By Josh McDowell and Dick Day (ROTF)
> *Is There Anything Wrong with Sex Before Marriage?* - Nicky Gumbel (ROTF)
> *No Sex Please (Until We're Married): The No-Compromise Search for the Love of Your Life* by Ian Gregory (ROTF)

Questions:

1. Do you feel its okay to live with your significant other before marriage? Why or why not?

....

....

....

Journal:

_____

....

_____

....

_____

....

_____

A DEEPER LOOK: CAKE ANYONE?

What was I doing there? I couldn't understand it. It was six a.m. and really cold out. I stepped out of my car and walked up to her apartment. She'd just gotten off work and I was going to take a nap with her before we spent the day together later. I was sure I would be strong and stay on top of the covers while she was underneath, but still, this wasn't me. . . .

I want you all to visualize in your mind the most delicious dessert you can think of. Got it? For me it's anything chocolate, but especially German Chocolate Cake. When it's around my "no sweets" diets quickly get thrown out the window, as all I can think of is that sweet taste in my mouth.

Now imagine you're famished and someone is treating you by taking you to your favorite restaurant. The server comes out with your food and also brings out your favorite dessert! How many of us are not going to want to grab that fork and bite into that dessert instead of waiting until we've finished the main meal? "Maybe just a taste," we think. I know my weaknesses—and chocolate is top on that list!

Is this type of temptation not what we do to ourselves when we are constantly alone with our significant other? We are so much more prone to failure when we are not careful about how and when we spend time together. Am I saying don't be alone together? No, definitely not. What I want to make you aware of though is that you are inviting trouble if you are not careful about this area of your life.

You see, the more you allow yourself these "small" things the more the "big things" get easier. Do you think people that have pre-marital sex start out in the beginning by saying, "Jessica, four months from now I think we should have sex." No! The world may talk this way, but most Christians do not.

What I want you to realize is that the beginning of a relationship is when you have the most resistance to failing in the area of purity. *This* is the time to make sure you have accountability. This is also the time to talk with the other person about when and how you will spend time together and what will be okay. Awkward perhaps? Well probably. But if this person is worth dating than that person will be strong enough to handle an awkward conversation with you.

Another thing to keep in mind is that guys and girls are built differently. Duh, right? We say that, but how many of us stop to think about what that means? If a girl gives a guy a kiss or holds his hand or cuddles with him, his mind is probably thinking, "sex, sex, sex!" It's inevitable; it's how guys are built. On the girl's end, though, most of them don't think exactly like that–their minds are focused elsewhere. For girls, it's more in "touch"–an embrace, soft touch, gentleness. It's not all touching and can be different for each girl, but generally "touches" make the girl feel closer to the guy and accepted. These are good things to keep in mind as it affects how that "big conversation" might go.

Do you think that four months down the line, when perhaps you have started experimenting with different things that you will be willing to start some accountability? Do you think you will want to have that "big conversation?" Of course not. When we are in sin, talking about it is the last thing we want to do. We'd rather rationalize, "pray" as usual, and keep going. Won't happen? Don't test yourself! Communicate early and often!

I challenge you today to start living a life of purity. Commit your relationships to God. Stay sexually pure. Dress in a way that is God-honoring, stay away from pornography, from fornication, from sex in movies and on television. Challenge the status quo that says these things are okay. Embrace God and His Word–He's waiting for you. All of us have failed in one way or another, but God wipes our slates clean when we ask Him to. The first step in moving on is confessing to God those sins that are keeping you from His throne. I John 1:9 says: "But if we confess our sins to Him, He is faithful and just to forgive us and to cleanse us from every wrong." Psalms 103:12: "He has removed our rebellious acts as far away from us as the east is from the west." Confess your sins and be willing to forget your past. Look to your future and decide what kind of choices you're going to make for yourself from now on.

"Come now, let us argue this out," says the Lord. "No matter how deep the stain of your sins, I can remove it. I can make you as clean as freshly fallen snow. Even if you are stained as red as crimson, I can make you as white as wool. If you will only obey me and let me help you, then you will have plenty to eat. But if you keep turning away and refusing to listen, you will have been destroyed by your enemies. I the Lord have spoken!" Isaiah 1:18–20

SUGGESTED READING FOR A DEEPER LOOK INTO THIS SUBJECT:

Dateable: Are you? Are they? by Justin Lookadoo and Hayley DiMarco
When God Writes Your Love Story by Eric & Leslie Ludy
Every Young Man's Battle series

Questions:

1. What's your favorite dessert? Can you imagine not eating it if it was in front of you, prepared just the way you like?

_____

_____

2. Who can you develop accountability with right now? Will you? More importantly, will you commit to being honest with them?

_____

_____

3. Will you commit now to "challenging the status quo" and dedicating yourself to a life of purity?

_____

A DEEPER LOOK: WHY DO BAD THINGS HAPPEN TO GOOD PEOPLE?

I sat down on the couch, completely dejected. The tears started flowing down my cheek, I couldn't help it. I'd just gotten off the phone with my bank and I was over a hundred dollars in the negative. Before that I'd checked on my credit cards and I was completely maxed to the tune of nine-thousand dollars. What was I going to do? I had no answers; my thoughts grew more negative. Suddenly my mind flashed to a bridge. I remembered it from a news report the other day. It was a long bridge that covered a huge gorge in the New Mexico desert. The news report was about how someone had driven their car right off the cliff. I thought to myself, "Now wouldn't that be easy. I could just . . . drive off . . . and it would be over. . . . no more problems. . . ."

That was a scary thought! I hated it but, I couldn't get it out of my head; the tears continued. Then I heard the front door open—my sister was home; it was time to put on a brave face . . .

It's impossible for us to know why some people are dealt a bad deck of cards. We all know people like that—you might be one of them. I know I have often wondered in the last year how God could let my friends have cancer and terminal illnesses when they were such good people. I have two such examples for you.

The first is my friend Dana. She's a middle-aged teacher with an outstanding family and a good life. Last year the doctors discovered she had cancer and they immediately did surgery to try to get rid of it. This was followed by months of agonizing chemotherapy in which she went into the doctor's office every other week and watched as they fed poison into her arm for hours. Thereafter she'd feel awful for days, only to repeat the cycle another week after she started to feel better. Now she is done with the chemotherapy and the doctors say she has a fifty-seven percent chance of living. I look at her life and wonder, "Why her?" She's an amazing woman and has been a wonderful friend in my life.

The second example is my friend Steve. He was my youth pas-

STEPHEN WINTERS

tor in my early years of college and I've been friend's with him ever since—even after they moved to another state. I lost track of him for a bit and when I caught up with him again I learned he had been diagnosed with ALS Disease. For those of you who don't know what that is, it's a terrible disease that ravages your nerves. It's a slow, agonizing way to die and most people who get it have less than five years to live. Steve is an outstanding guy who has done wonderful things for the kingdom of God—so again I ask, "Why him?" He has a wonderful little boy who is an amazing kid and I wonder what it might be like for him to grow up without his father.

Such wonderful people—how have they moved beyond this? I think both have learned to look at this world with an eternal perspective that defies normal logic. Both see this world as a fallen world that they are merely passing through. They see their job as doing whatever they can and using this in whatever way they can.

They are both tough people—tough in that their faith was strong enough to handle this. Did God give them these illnesses? I don't know—I'm definitely not wise enough to have the answer to that. I do know that God can use anything for His eternal plans and that both these people have already and will continue to affect many people for Christ.

I began today's reading with a story that represented some of the lowest points in my life during my time in New Mexico. My concerns were mostly financial—mixed in with some serious God-doubts and acute loneliness. Have you ever had moments like these, where suicide seems like a nice easy way out? I'm sure we all have in one way or another.

For those of you who have lived those times I want to offer you a passage that has helped me. It's found in Romans 5:1–5:

Therefore, since we have been made right in God's sight by faith, we have peace with God because of what Jesus Christ our Lord has done for us. Because of our faith, Christ has brought us into this place of highest privilege where we now stand, and we confidently and joyfully look forward to sharing God's glory. We can rejoice, too, when we run into problems and trials, for we know that they are good for us—they help us learn to endure. And endurance develops strength of character in us, and character strengthens our confident expectation of salvation. And this expectation will not disappoint us. For we know how dearly God loves us, because he has given us the Holy Spirit to fill our hearts with his love.

Why does God allow suffering? This passage offers us one reason—so He can mold us into stronger Christians. Is that enough of an answer for you? I doubt it and that's why I suggest reading some more books and seeking out God's answer through Scripture. I've talked with enough people to know that this is one of those questions that has no cut and dry answer. The argument / evidence that brings you to a point of acceptance may mean absolutely nothing to someone else. In the end, I think it comes down to a choice. Both Dana and Steve have chosen to make the best of their situation. Though I know both of them struggle with the answers, they've chosen to do what they can in using it for His glory.

I want to leave you with the example of Job. If you've never heard the story of Job he was a rich landowner in ancient times who is known for having his faith tested in an extreme way. Satan claimed to God that the only reason Job loved God was because God had made him a very rich man. So God allowed Satan to take everything away from Job to see what Job's reaction would be. His land, his belongings, and even his children were all taken away from him. When Satan covered Job's body with horrible sores and his wife told him to curse God and die, still Job would not turn against Him. I don't think Job thought he had all the answers either. He got through his extreme adversity with an unshakable faith that God was indeed in control.

When are you feeling your lowest? Perhaps you might try to find someone else to pour some love into. You will feel great for lifting them up and your time of trial will pass. Have you ever seen the acronym JOY? It breaks down to Jesus, Others, Yourself. This should be how our priorities stack out anyway. Remember I said that we exist for God's glory? Well He is very clear about how we are to go about doing that. Mark 12 tells us that the greatest commandment is to love the Lord your God with all your heart, soul, mind, and strength. The second greatest commandment is to love our neighbors as we do ourselves. These verses validate the JOY acronym very well—wouldn't you agree?

➡ "THERE ARE EVILS THAT HAVE THE ABILITY TO SURVIVE IDENTIFICATION AND GO ON FOR EVER . . . MONEY, FOR INSTANCE, OR WAR."

~SAUL BELLOW

➡ "THERE HAS TO BE EVIL SO THAT GOOD CAN PROVE ITS PURITY ABOVE IT."

~BUDDHA

➡ "THERE IS NO EXPLANATION FOR EVIL. IT MUST BE LOOKED UPON AS A NECESSARY PART OF THE ORDER OF THE UNIVERSE. TO IGNORE IT IS CHILDISH, TO BEWAIL IT SENSELESS."

~W. SOMERSET MAUGHAM

➡ "SATAN TREMBLES WHEN HE SEES THE WEAKEST SAINT UPON THEIR KNEES."

~WILLIAM COWPER

SUGGESTED READING FOR A DEEPER LOOK INTO THIS SUBJECT:

The Problem of Pain by C.S. Lewis

God, Freedom, and Evil by Alvin Plantinga (ROTF)

Making Sense Out of Suffering by Peter Kreeft (ROTF)

Suffering and God by Alister McGrath (ROTF)

How Long, O Lord?: Reflections on Evil and Suffering by D.A. Carson (ROTF)

No Easy Answers: Finding Hope in Doubt, Failure, and Unanswered Prayer by William Lane Craig (ROTF)

Questions:

1. What kind of tough times has God put in your life? Have you ever considered suicide? What led you to those thoughts? What kept you going?

_____

_____

_____

2. Will you try to change your outlook on life to match what we are told in Mark 12? Will you act out the JOY acronym?

_____

_____

_____

Journal:

_____

_____

_____

_____

_____

_____

_____

_____

_____

_____

_____

A DEEPER LOOK: WHY SHOULD I BELIEVE IN THE BIBLE OR EVEN HAVE A FAITH?

Dear Lord, Why should I even care any more? This book doesn't even make sense, where are YOU in all of this? I want to believe, but I have doubts. So many doubts. . . .

I'm not going to spend too much time on this section because I'd have to write a whole other book before I would even come close to answering it enough. There are other men who have done that and I suggest you read what they've written—you'll see a few suggestions later.

I just want to talk for a minute about the words "leap of faith." No matter how informed you are, in the end, in order to find Christ, you must make a leap of faith. If you read the writings of Billy Graham he talks about that. As a young man new in the ministry he had considerable doubts. One day he realized he was going to have to live with some of those doubts as they lacked definitive answers. He told God he was going to accept the grace of God and believe fully in Him despite his nagging questions. From that day forward he was placing absolute faith in God. The rest is history.

To some it seems that the Bible is full of contradictions. For instance, if the Bible is truly inspired, why do the narratives in the gospels not fully align with the other gospels? There are others—a simple search on the internet with the words "Biblical contradictions" will lead you to sites filled with them. In the end, though, there is more leading me to faith, and even faith in the Bible, than away from it.

I believe that it takes more faith to be an agnostic or atheist then to have faith in God. There is clearly a superior being that fashioned this world. All I have to do is drive into the mountains and view the majesty of nature to know that. For me the more I study the Bible, the more I realize how much I don't know and how much more I want to learn. I see the potential for error and I think it's important for us to realize that the versions we read have gone through many translations–human translations. There is the potential that every word I read in the Bible may not be completely accurate, but I also strongly believe in the role of the Holy Spirit. We could read the same passage two different times and the Holy Spirit might "teach" us something totally different both times. I believe part of the role of the Holy Spirit is to guide us to a true understanding of God and His teachings through what we read and the interactions in our daily lives.

As for faith, I suggest reading *Mere Christianity* by C.S. Lewis. It can be a bit heavy at times, but Lewis has a way of bringing it all together so stick with him. He is able to argue for the existence of God and the need for faith without even mentioning God in the first quarter of his book. Amazing? Yeah, I'd say so.

Whatever your situation and whatever doubts you may have, I pray you will never stop searching Him out. We all go through periods of doubt and you will probably have many more throughout your lifetime. The important thing is to keep searching and be willing to learn. Learning usually means growing, and I pray God will guide you on your path.

SUGGESTED READING FOR A DEEPER LOOK INTO THIS SUBJECT:

The Case For Faith by Lee Strobel

Mere Christianity by C.S. Lewis

The Shaping of Things to Come by Michael Frost and Alan Hirsch

Questions:

1. Have you ever doubted the existence of God? Have you ever wondered, "Why should I believe?" Talk about those experiences.

LEARN AND MOVE ON

This chapter is about something very few of us ever truly learn to do: Learn from our past and move on. So often we let our mistakes continue haunting us long after we supposedly achieved forgiveness. We're going to look at some verses and see a few examples of God's approach to our past failures.

LEARN AND MOVE ON: WE SCREWED UP, WHAT NOW?

➡ "I HAVE ALWAYS FELT THAT ALTHOUGH SOMEONE MAY DE-FEAT ME, AND I STRIKE OUT IN A BALL GAME, THE PITCHER ON THE PARTICULAR DAY WAS THE BEST PLAYER. BUT I KNOW WHEN I SEE HIM AGAIN, I'M GOING TO BE READY FOR HIS CURVE BALL. FAILURE IS A PART OF SUCCESS. THERE IS NO SUCH THING AS A BED OF ROSES ALL YOUR LIFE. BUT FAILURE WILL NEVER STAND IN THE WAY OF SUCCESS IF YOU LEARN FROM IT."

~HANK AARON

➡ "MY DOWNFALL RAISES ME TO INFINITE HEIGHTS."

~NAPOLEON BONAPARTE

➡ "FAILURE IS AN EVENT, NEVER A PERSON."

~WILLIAM D. BROWN

➡ "YOU DON'T DROWN BY FALLING IN THE WATER; YOU DROWN BY STAYING THERE."

~EDWIN LOUIS COLE

So . . . you screwed up–now what? Every one of us is a sinner–Ro-

mans 3:23 confirms that: "For all have sinned and fall short of the glory of God." (NASB) So why then do you refuse to allow yourself to move on from your past? You think, "There is no way God could truly forgive me for *this*." You pretend to ask God for forgiveness but deep inside you nurse your wounds and make them your crutch. You even build huge walls that keep people out because you think they couldn't truly love what you really are. Tomorrow we are going to take a look at several people in the Bible and see how God responded to them. I'm only asking one question today. It is important to figure out what it is that keeps you from moving forward, so I want you to have plenty of time to think it through.

Questions:

1. Reflecting on your past, what things / past experiences are you harboring in your heart that are keeping you from a right communion with God?

_____

_____

_____

Journal:

_____

_____

_____

_____

_____

_____

_____

LEARN AND MOVE ON: WE'RE NOT THE ONLY ONES?

"Moses stuttered. David's armor didn't fit. John Mark was rejected by Paul. Hosea's wife was a prostitute. Amos' only training was in the school of fig tree pruning. Jacob was a liar. David had an affair and had the husband killed. Solomon was too rich and Abraham was too old. Jeremiah and David were too young and Timothy had ulcers. Peter was afraid of death and Lazarus was dead. John was self-righteous and Jesus was homeless. Naomi was a widow and Ruth was a foreigner. Paul and Moses were murderers. Jonah ran from God. Miriam was a gossip and Gideon and Thomas both doubted. Jeremiah was depressed and suicidal. Elijah was burned out and John the Baptist was a loudmouth. Martha was a type A personality and her sister Mary was lazy. Samson had long hair and Noah got drunk. Moses had a short fuse—so did Peter, Paul, and many others." ~ Unknown source

America is a country of individuals. When it comes down to it we all have a dynamite sense of national pride. However, as we move about our daily lives I think most of us would admit it's all about us. We think the world revolves around us and we live our life accordingly.

We do the same thing with our hurts and failures. We think we are the only ones that have gone through that particular issue and use it as an excuse to continue the cycle. We must break free of it! We must stop making mountains out of molehills. As I've said in a previous chapter, do not mock God's forgiveness! The world is filled with people who won't break free of the bonds of this perpetuating lifestyle—will you?

We need to realize that we are not the only ones! The Bible is filled with people who made mistakes—yet God was able to use them anyway! Need proof—just look at the list provided earlier, and that list isn't even a complete one.

Let's take just two examples, David and Paul. David, from the time he was a boy, was used by God. He wrestled lions, kept his father's sheep and generally had more faith than the entire army of Israel as he alone killed Goliath. God called him a man after His own heart! Yet this is a man who had an affair with another man's wife and later had that man killed. Wow—a life of opposites to say the least. The same could be said of Paul. He was the biggest persecutor of Jews for many years—a murderer for a large part of his life. Yet he later became the greatest apostle / evangelist to ever live!

God used these men for great things and He can use you too! One thing we must keep in our minds is to remain humble. As my pastor would say, "sin is sin is sin!" There are no levels to sin so just because we have not murdered another man does not mean we are better than someone who has. Remember in God's eyes once we have been cleansed by the blood of the cross we are all equal!

I love the story of the prodigal son. For those of you who've never read it, please do (Luke 15:11–32). I think this story sums up our culture in a nutshell: why get it later when we can have it now? Do you think the prodigal son set out to waste his inheritance and live a meaningless existence? Do you think he said one day, "I think I'm going to go as far away as I can, blow all my money, and end up eating pig slop." I think not! It's all a progression—a series of choices. Why are we in such a hurry? Why do we rush through life and let the joys and real meanings pass us by? Don't be in a hurry to get rid of your youth. Learn the lesson the prodigal son learned and enjoy your youth while you can.

The story is a great parable. Just as the father of this young man welcomes him back with open arms so does our Father when we stray. How awesome to know that we have this type of love in our lives no matter how bad things seem!

Questions:

1. Think of a an example from the Bible or your own personal life where God used someone for His kingdom after they had made a huge mistake / sin:

_____

_____

STEPHEN WINTERS

2. Look back at your answer from our question in day one. Have you forgiven yourself fully for this error? Has God? If you are unable to forgive yourself completely, will you talk to someone about this today?

_____

_____

_____

Journal:

_____

_____

_____

_____

_____

_____

_____

_____

_____

_____

_____

_____

_____

_____

_____

_____

_____

LEARN AND MOVE ON: THE NEXT STEP

➡ "A LEADER IS SOMEONE WHO HELPS IMPROVE THE LIVES OF
OTHER PEOPLE OR IMPROVE THE SYSTEM THEY LIVE UN-
DER."

~SAM ERVIN

We messed up and we're learning to move on—where do we go
from here? Maybe you could teach someone about your journey!
God has not allowed you to pass through your trials for nothing. It
is His desire that you find a way to use your experience for Him.
Look around you. Most likely there is someone who can benefit
from the mistakes you've made. This is what churches so easily
miss. We can become so concentrated on reaching out to our community or evangelizing that we forget about our fellow Christians.
What better place than a church to find that person who needs
you? Do you think that everyone in your church has got it together? You can find hurting people anywhere . . .

Here's the way I believe God intended the church to work: we
were put here on this earth for God's glory and God's glory alone.
I've talked about this before in other chapters. The way we do
that is through His two greatest commandments—to love God and
to love others in our every thought, word, and deed. I believe He
intends for us to first do that in our churches. The church is where
we practice what we need to be to the world. The church is the
backbone of our faith. Without the church and the support of each
other how can we survive? Paul needed the church in this way.

We cannot allow ourselves to lose the focus that God intended
us to have. We must act in the true spirit of fellowship before we can
ever conquer the world for Him. Why do people come to churches
and not get involved? Why do they stay on the sidelines? Why is
it that young people (youth to young adults) bounce from church
to church—remaining faceless people? Because we are all looking
for something few of us ever find. We want to be at a church that
embraces this concept of true fellowship

Let us become like these people who follow Jesus! The best

place you can learn to use your failures, trials, and experiences is in the church! Find someone around you who you can start mentoring. Or perhaps you might just become their friend and give them the listening ear they need. Few of us are very good at opening up, especially when it comes to things we'd rather keep buried in our past. God doesn't want that though! Of course there are some things better left in the past, but we must get to the point where we can use our experiences for His good! Let me encourage you to stretch yourself. See what you are comfortable with and then continue to stretch yourself just a little bit farther. You will be amazed at how God will use you in ways you never dreamed possible! Not only that, you will also be amazed at how much more comforted you feel after you realize that God did bring good out of your trials!

I know! I was the guy who wasn't supposed to fail. Seriously, I come from a long line of people in the ministry. My mom's dad was a Baptist preacher. My dad's dad was a Baptist missionary to Japan. I was born in Japan as my dad and mom also became missionaries there. Even my brother and his family are back in Japan as missionaries now. I look back at where I've screwed up the most and I wonder how I got there. I am not one to live in the past though and neither should you! Sure, feelings of guilt or regret can get to you. We are human after all. If we've really given these things to God though those feelings go away and they should be replaced with a desire to use those experiences for Him. I believe it's a natural progression and the way God intended it to be. So look for the opportunities–He will use you!

Questions:

1. What failures, trails, or experiences in your past do you feel God can use for His good right now?

_____

_____

2. Who do you know that you can be used by God to bring comfort too?

_____

_____

_____

3. Will you commit to praying at least three times a week asking God to bring people into your life that you can bring comfort too?

_____

_____

🏔️ Journal:

_____

_____

_____

_____

_____

_____

_____

_____

_____

_____

_____

_____

_____

_____

_____

ADDICTION

This chapter is being added at the last minute because I think it's that important. Addictions keep Christians from being effective in their walk. I've struggled with an addiction for quite some time, and I now see it for what it is.

ADDICTION: LITTLE WORD, BIG PROBLEM . . .

March 4, 2006 11:34 p.m.

I'm addicted to gambling—Texas Hold Em. There, I said it. Why has it taken me a year and several thousand dollars to figure this out? I'm tired of my excuses and I'm tired of the endless way I rationalize it in my mind. The money isn't hurting me and I'm having fun. Or so I say. I wish I could find a way to play the game and not lose—but there is another rationalization. One of the problems is I'm good at the game—just good enough that I can win big a few times to make me want to stick around. But then there are those bad nights—the nights where the cards will absolutely not come. I admire the people with enough self control to just leave. I'm not that controlled yet. Sometimes I am, but "sometimes" is not good enough. I don't like what it's doing to me. I don't like that it makes me want to cuss more. Most of all I hate the feeling that I don't have complete control of my life. I've always been in control of everything. Actually, as I write this I think I finally understand why it's been so hard to give full control of my life to God. Things run better when I do, but it's hard for my mind to comprehend that fully because I'm a control freak. So how could I let myself lose perspective on this game? I wish I never would have sat down at my first table. I did though, and now I need to do something about it. I've tried putting a sign up on my wall and briefly telling a few people about this, but it hasn't been enough. I know the biggest issue is surrendering this thing fully to God. It's funny, the answers are staring me in the face, yet I still don't want to see it. I think it's time to try. . . .

What I have to talk to you about today is so important - words can't adequately express just how much. This subject is timeless and intense . . . and personal. If this book hasn't already demonstrated how open I'm willing to be if it will help you live a more God-filled life, this chapter should.

Addiction. One word, a word that strikes more fear into my heart than I've ever known. You see, I'm addicted. It's taken me forever to admit it, but now I see it. Finally. I've lost thousands upon thousands of dollars at casino tables and I haven't even been to Las Vegas. I have a great job and a book contract, but I'm more terrified about finances right now than I've ever been. This should be one of the most exciting times in my life—instead I'm wracked by intense desires to be back on the tables, always thinking that I can make the money back on the next game.

I've said this before—sin is fun. It was fun when I was having sex before marriage, it was fun when I was cussing up a storm in an attempt to be one of the guys, it was fun when I was playing on those poker tables—the list goes on and on. (By the way, The Bible does talk about gambling, but that's not the point of this chapter.) Here is the kicker though, and what you really need to pay attention to—sin is fun, but there are always consequences!

It may not be right away, but sin always has a way of catching up to you. Often in the moment, you can skate around it, ignore it, or delay it, but in the end it will always come back to haunt you. A significant number of you know what I'm talking about because you have already dealt with consequences or are dealing with them now. The rest of you will soon—it's inescapable.

Now that we've agreed sin has consequences, let's dive deeper into the subject of addiction. Addictions can become as much a part of you as each breath you take. They take over your life and strongly influence your decisions. They choke the good desires and force us to make bad decisions. I know, I've been making bad decisions for months now.

It would be easy for us to blame bad decisions on addictions and leave it at that, continuing down the road to ruin. How long would it be though before we had no Christian character left at all? If you are struggling with an addiction I want you to know that you are not the only one. I am struggling with my addiction and there are thousands of other Christians just like us. I know married men who struggle with pornography on a daily basis and Christian leaders in the church who struggle with many things, from cussing to movies to other far worse issues.

I don't tell you this to make you doubt the leaders in your church, but to show you that we are all human and deal with the same world and many of the same struggles. I've no doubt that every one of you are dealing with at least a mild addiction to something. Pornography, selfish desires, drugs, alcohol, masturbation, sex, video games, gambling, movies—the list goes on and only you know which ones apply to you.

The important thing is not only that you recognize it, but that you do something about it. Recognition is not enough. Every time I left a casino after another all-nighter I knew that what I was doing to myself was wrong. It disgusted me how I could frivolously toss so much money away and barely be conscious of doing it. I would cry out to God every time to do something that would keep me from going back. I'd wonder how such a "smart" and savvy financial person could throw so much money away.

The answer? Addictions change us into people we don't want to be. The person who used to make smart financial decisions was now making stupid ones several times a month. When I was on those poker tables I completely lost track of who I was. I didn't realize how much poker had changed me, and I refuse to be that person any longer.

That sounds like a very adamant statement, right? You would say, "Stephen definitely won't mess up again because he's made a very conscious choice to not screw up anymore." Wrong. I'm as scared as ever that I will be back on those poker tables tomorrow night, the next night, or perhaps the following night. The answers then are not as simple as making a choice. Tomorrow we will discuss what the answers are.

Questions:

1. Be honest with yourself—what addictions are you struggling with in your life today?

_____

_____

_____

Journal:

_____

_____

_____

_____

_____

_____

_____

_____

_____

_____

_____

_____

ADDICTION: THE ANSWERS

MY PRAYER JOURNAL

By Jennifer Hoadley (personal friend)

When I knelt to pray tonight, there's something I have to admit,
I felt no desire to talk with God, no, not really one little bit.
But as I brought this to the Lord, asking Him to change my heart,
I pushed aside thoughts of myself,
opened my journal, and began to start,
going down my list of prayers for people that I knew,
bringing each one before the Lord, and trusting He knew what to do.
As time and words went on my heart began to feel,
As I fervently lifted them up to God, I regained a passion that is so real.
It seems sort of ironic now, when I look back on that time and see,
that as I asked Him to work in others, He was also working in me.

I believe the choice to change is the biggest part of the solution, but as I said before, recognition of your addiction is not enough to get over it. It takes more. I'll give you an example. What I didn't tell you about the passage at the beginning of yesterday's lesson is that it was written several months earlier than this passage. In those months I've continued to screw up in ways that I never could have imagined I would. I've lost thousands more on the poker tables and have become far more addicted to the game. I've kept up a pretense with all my friends–there are few people in my life who even know I play at all. I've missed outings with friends and family and not been places I should have been. I've learned to be a very good chameleon and I've been even better at giving evasive answers about my whereabouts. Really, the FBI would be so proud of me–I was quite the double agent.

In short, I've missed out on a lot of life and put myself into a financial hole that I must now dig myself out of. I will survive financially and come out again on top–IF I can learn to stay away from the casinos for good. Beyond the finances, though, I'm more disappointed in the person I've become and the moments of life I can't get back. I've told you guys before that I think regrets are a form of not learning from the past, so I choose to learn from all of this. What I've learned is this—we must DO something about our addictions. I'll tell you what I've done and perhaps it will illustrate what I mean.

First, I have talked to God and asked His forgiveness for my actions. Next, I've "locked" my credit and debit cards in such a way that will make it harder to gamble. Lastly, I've set up accountability with people who know me that will ask about this specific issue in my life. I've asked them to ask me about it and then to ask me if I'm lying. It's one thing to lie to someone, but it's a lot harder to lie to them about lying!

Does that tell you what must be done? Without reconciliation with Christ, everything else you do is pointless, so that must be the first step. After that it is very important that you set up proper accountability with people you trust that will help you with whatever issue you are facing. If you don't know anyone, pray about it and God will show you the answer. These two things may not be enough though. Whatever you are facing, it may be very important that you do something else. For me it was not giving myself access to money beyond my bills. Perhaps for you it is the same thing—you may need to change the friends you have or walk home a different way than the one that leads you by the liquor store you buy your pornography from, or maybe you need to get out of a relationship that is dragging you down through sexual temptation.

Whatever you do, do something. The more you talk with God about it, the more you stay accountable to friends, and the more you try—the better your chances of overcoming your addictions and living the Christian life you want. Don't let addictions control your life and please don't be afraid to ask for help. By the way, you may want to look at www.faithdango.com. It's a resource center that I've pioneered to help teenagers with specific needs. It can be a great place to start on the road to recovery.

You may wonder why I've been so personal in this chapter. In some ways you could say I've used you all by making you all

174

partners in my accountability. If I met any of you at a casino now, I'd have a hard time explaining why I was there. You face a much harder task. You may be addicted and no one knows about it at all. I'm not saying you need to tell everyone and their mother. I am saying that it will be a lot easier to overcome it if you confide in someone. Admitting you need help is never an easy thing, but I hope you will take the time to try.

Questions:

1. Will you commit to overcoming your addictions through prayer and accountability? Will you commit to doing what it takes?

_____

_____

_____

Journal:

_____

_____

_____

_____

_____

_____

_____

_____

_____

_____

_____

_____

_____

CONCLUSION

You know, one of the reasons I included the previous chapter was to show you that I'm still struggling in the trenches just like you. Sometimes I have trouble living by one of my life mottos "let go, let God." I don't claim to have all the answers and my goal in writing this book was certainly not to come off as a know-it-all. So . . . for those of you who find yourself struggling through some of life's obstacles, I'd like to offer these final words of encouragement that come straight from Scriptures:

God always provides a way out of any and every temptation He puts into your life. Ecclesiastes 8: 5b-6:

Those who are wise will find a time and a way to do what is right. Yes, there is a time and a way for everything, even as people's troubles lie heavily upon them."

The wisdom we need to make even ordinary decisions comes from reading the Bible. Psalms 119: 97–105:

Oh, how I love your law! I think about it all day long. Your commands make me wiser than my enemies; for your commands are my constant guide. Yes, I have more insight than my teachers, for I am always thinking of your decrees. I am even wiser than my elders, for I have kept your commandments. I have refused to walk on any path of evil, that I may remain obedient to your word. I haven't turned away from your laws, for you have taught me well. How sweet are your words to my taste; they are sweeter than honey. Your commandments give me understanding; no wonder I hate every false way of life. Your word is a lamp for my feet, and a light for my path.

Patience, no matter how difficult, is a quality that all of us should strive for. All of Psalms 37 affirms this but for space I've targeted verse 5 through 9:

Commit everything you do to the Lord. Trust in him, and he will help you. He will make your innocence as clear as the dawn, and the justice of your cause will shine like the noonday sun. Be still in the presence of the Lord, and wait patiently for him to act. Don't worry about evil people who prosper or fret about their wicked schemes. Stop your anger! Turn from your rage! Do not envy others-it only leads to harm. For the wicked will be destroyed, but those who trust in the Lord will possess the land.

Success is difficult to achieve without accountability. Philippians 2:12–15:

Dearest friends, you were always so careful to follow my instructions when I was with you. And now that I am away you must be even more careful to put into action God's saving work in your lives, obeying God with deep reverence and fear. For God is working in you, giving you the desire to obey him and the power to do what pleases him. In everything you do, stay away from complaining and arguing, so that no one can speak a word of blame against you. You are to live clean, innocent lives as children of God in a dark world full of crooked and perverse people. Let your lives shine brightly before them.

Start small! Making promises to God you can't keep sets yourself up for failure. Ecclesiastes 5: 2–6:

And don't make rash promises to God, for he is in heaven, and you are only here on earth. So let your words be few. Just as being too busy gives you nightmares, being a fool makes you a blabbermouth.

So when you make a promise to God, don't delay in following through, for God takes no pleasure in fools. Keep all the promises you make to him. It is better to say nothing than to promise something that you don't follow through on.

There is a time for everything; try not to be so rushed that you forget to act on God's leading in your life. Ecclesiastes 3: 1–8:

There is a time for everything, a season for every activity under heaven. A time to be born and a time to die. A time to plant and a time to harvest. A time to kill and a time to heal. A time to tearn down and a time to rebuild. A time to cry and a time to laugh. A time to grieve and a time to dance. A time to scatter stones and a time to gather stones. A time to embrace and a time to turn away. A time to search and a time to lose. A time to keep and a time to throw away. A time to tear and a time to mend. A time to be quiet and a time to speak up. A time to love and a time to hate. A time for war and a time for peace.

Can you imagine if Paul had spent all his time worrying about his past mistakes how little he would have done for the Kingdom of God? You can't let past mistakes keep you from achieving what God wants you to achieve. Once you've confessed your sins God has forgiven you. I John 1:9: "But if we confess our sins to him, he is faithful and just to forgive us and to cleanse us from every wrong."

Be real! Nothing is more contagious than someone who has a genuine light for Christ, free from hypocrisy! So many of us have failed in trying to achieve that–will you try?

Know that God is your ultimate source of validation! You must learn to love yourself as you are–God's creation. I believe you cannot truly love another until you learn to love yourself.

Someday, when I'm on my deathbed ready to pass from this world to the next, I hope my last words can be similar to Paul's:

"As for me, my life has already been poured out as an offering to

God. The time of my death is near. I have fought a good fight, I have finished the race, and I have remained faithful." (2 Timothy 4: 6–8)

CONSIDER THIS QUOTE: Care more than others think is wise, risk more than others think is safe, dream more than others think is practical, expect more than others think is possible!

MAY GOD BLESS YOU ALL IN YOUR EFFORTS!

STEPHEN WINTERS

ABOUT THE AUTHOR

AUTHOR STEPHEN WINTERS was born in Japan where his grandparents and parents were missionaries. When Stephen was two his family moved from Japan to Southern California where he grew up. He graduated with his bachelor's degree in Interdisciplinary Studies from Cascade College in Portland, Oregon, in 2006. His greatest passion is sharing and encouraging action-based faith in teens across the nation and world. He is also the founder of www.faith-dango.com, an online resource center for teens.

TATE PUBLISHING *& Enterprises*

Tate Publishing is committed to excellence in the publishing industry. Our staff of highly trained professionals, including editors, graphic designers, and marketing personnel, work together to produce the very finest books available. The company reflects the philosophy established by the founders, based on Psalms 68:11,

"THE LORD GAVE THE WORD AND GREAT WAS THE COMPANY
OF THOSE WHO PUBLISHED IT."

If you would like further information, please call
1.888.361.9473
or visit our website
www.tatepublishing.com

TATE PUBLISHING *& Enterprises*, LLC
127 E. Trade Center Terrace
Mustang, Oklahoma 73064 USA